Andrew J. Smith, J. P. Watson

The Light of Other Days

Passing under the Rod

Andrew J. Smith, J. P. Watson

The Light of Other Days
Passing under the Rod

ISBN/EAN: 9783337812997

Printed in Europe, USA, Canada, Australia, Japan

Cover: Foto ©Thomas Meinert / pixelio.de

More available books at **www.hansebooks.com**

THE

LIGHT OF OTHER DAYS;

OR,

PASSING UNDER THE ROD,

BY

ELDER A. J. SMITH.

Edited by REV. J. P. WATSON.

DAYTON, OHIO
United Brethren Publishing House,
1878.

TO MY MOTHER,

THAN WHOM IN REAL WORTH

THE WORLD HATH NEVER SEEN

A BETTER, A DEARER, NOR A TRUER MOTHER,

IS THIS HUMBLE STORY OF A LIFE

GRATEFULLY DEDICATED,

AS A SIMPLE TOKEN OF

WARMEST AND MOST MERITED LOVE,

BY HER SON,

THE AUTHOR.

PREFACE.

The thought of writing a book wherein should be told the simple story of my unimportant life has but recently suggested itself. Truly the motive has not been ambition, nor the end sought the selfish one of fame. I care not how soon my humble name may perish, if from its ashes there would earlier spring a wreath of glory for my Master's name.

If the world asks an apology for my temerity, I give it in the simple wish to inspire some drooping, fainting soul with fresher life by the example of my own. If I have magnified my follies, it is that the forbearance and mercies of my Lord may appear, and if my blessings, only that the goodness of the Father may be seen.

As Milton's daughter took the story of "Paradise Lost" from the lips of her blind and sainted father, so has my story been patiently sketched from my lips by my generous friend and brother, Rev. J. P. Watson, whom I gratefully present to the reader as the editor of this unvarnished work. May the reader find here a fountain that shall yield one cooling, refreshing draught at least, and a table on which a few crumbs of nourishing bread shall be found. Indeed, that at least a single soul shall find peace in believing and sweet rest in Christ from its perusal I humbly ask as a boon from Heaven. This much, and the author's toil, hath ample compensation.

Though in blindness I have sown these humble seeds, yet with clearest vision shall I wield the sickle in the harvest morn. May you and I be reapers with the angels.

A. J. S.

Pleasant Hill, Ohio, October, 1876.

CONTENTS.

CHAPTER I.

In the eastern part of the State of Pennsylvania, to the northward of its great city—the nation's Centennial center and birth-place—a distance of forty miles, and to the westward of the bold, bluffy Delaware some four miles, in one of the most romantic and beautiful sections of the state, stood the old-fashioned farm-house of Esquire Smith, my honored grandfather. It was, as I recollect, a stately stone mansion, and roomy enough for the children of a generation. A flood of light illumed the interior through a long, encircling row of windows, and from above by several dormer-windows, as if the good old man would catch the first light from heaven and have a nearer view of the worlds above.

Its roominess entitled the mansion to be called a hospitable home, and served somewhat to illustrate this most excellent quality of the owner's heart. While there was ample room within, there was also plenty of elbow-room without, both in

front and rear. It did not, like so many and too
many modern homes where comfort and conven-
ience are claimed to be a chief aim and end, crowd
the very street; but, with a large, open, and tasteful lawn in front, it presented to all the appearance
of comfort, liberty, and generosity. The man who
will crowd himself will be niggardly toward others; and this pinching habit is too often suffered
about our homes. The worshipful heart of my
grandsire typified its vigorous hold on the divine
hand by the towering reach-heavenward of the
giant poplars to the south of his home. While
their heads reached to a dizzy hight, as if they
would be crowned by down-reaching hands from
on high, their strong, broad arms seemed as if anxious to embrace the blessed brotherhood of earth,
and lift their souls above.

The surrounding scenery, as fashioned by Nature's artistic hand, was beautiful beyond description, while with the warble of feathered songsters
old Delaware mingled the music of its roar, as if
offering praise to its Creator. These beautiful surroundings had their crown from God's own hand
in the majestic Haycock Mountains, a few miles to
the west. These, as if to add new glory to the
scene, to speak anew their Maker's praise, and bring
a benediction upon the voice of song ere the nightly shades should deepen, would reflect the golden

rays of the king of dying day as he bowed his
crowned head into the mystic deeps beyond.

There was a voice of inspiration in this vision;
and it failed not to awaken a spirit of grateful inspiration in the heart of William Smith. He would
not detract from, but add to the beauty and grandeur of the whole by adding new charms to Nature's
work. The wild beauty he tamed, and softened
with his touch the general grandeur of the Maker's
works. Adam, though in the garden, was appointed to dress and cultivate it; and so here a
worthy son would aid Nature in her efforts at display, and bring more sunlight upon the scenes of
native beauty.

My grandfather was a large, vigorous man, with
stalwart frame, massive head, and shaggy locks, but
with a countenance like an open window for the
soul within. Some souls seem barred behind not
grates alone, but cold, rugged shutters, as if they
would receive no outward light and suffer no ray
to beam forth from the throne within. The tenant
of the earthly tabernacle, like the inmate of a
dwelling, should not seek to hide himself from the
eye of the world; but, standing at the window, as
it were, the soul should look forth and greet the
brotherhood of life. An open countenance is a
grand possession; and if nature has shaded it the
soul should, by cultivation, unlock and unbolt its

bars and throw open its shutters. Let the sunlight of nature in, and that of humanity and love will bloom out.

But with Wm. Smith the beaming face was not alone. It was not enough with him that beams of sunshine should gladden the paths of others. The willing, generous hand was full of benefactions to the worthy. He neither passed worth nor want without recognition for the one and aid for the other. His personal worth was witnessed by his neighbors in the honors with which they crowned him. For thirty or more years he dispensed justice with an impartial heart, and defended the honor of the law of the land. He delighted, as a peace-maker, to pull down those barriers that separated heart from heart and help untie knots of naughty dispute.

Many youthful hearts, however, he entangled in meshes from which they could not easily be disentangled. The nuptial knot was a matter of delight with him; and few could tie it better or were more popular in the effort of it. With the binding word he would give the seal of a cordial kiss, which, whatever the judgment of the bride, was a feast to himself. He had in the direction of marriage set the youth a goodly example by at an early age taking to himself and his home one of the fair ones of earth.

Of Mary Darrah, the chosen bride of my grandfather, I know but little. She was, however, in every way worthy of a most worthy man. She was the daughter of a wealthy farmer of the neighborhood, and was accounted both handsome and hearty. With a heart to love, she brought a good, strong hand to help the companion of her choice. With an ambition in keeping with her natural health, she shrunk from no toil that could bring comfort to the heart or ease to the weary hand of her husband. By mutual toil they earned their home and accumulated their fortune; and by the blessing of a gracious Providence through long life they enjoyed it together. The angel of death, indeed, came first for him, but she tarried only a little while on this hither shore. Soon they were together again, and forever *one* in their home above.

CHAPTER II.

MY GRANDFATHER'S FAMILY.

Seven children came of this union, three of whom were boys. Samuel, the oldest son, was of the Jackson school of politics, and gave his life almost wholly to this department of labor. His triumphant successes, perhaps, kept full pace with his ripening ambition. In the home military service he rose to the rank of general, while in civil life, from the seat of a county judge he finally came to occupy the honorable position of congressman from his district.

Robert was less ambitious, but honored, nevertheless, as his father had been, by home offices of trust and worth.

William, my father, remained at the old homestead until upward of forty years of age, having the general care of the family and superintendence of the farm-work. Being an excellent scribe, he finally obtained an official position at the county seat, where the methods and habits of his life became somewhat changed. Here he formed the acquaintance of his future wife, my mother, a Miss

Catherine Martin. She was a young lady of humble parentage, and at a tender age left her home for adoption in a farmer's family, where she remained until of age. She then removed to Doylestown, and became an inmate of the family of Rev. Dr. Andrews, pastor of the Old School Presbyterian Church. Of Dr. Andrews we shall have occasion to speak more at length hereafter. Here she found a good home, and received the best of religious instruction. She soon entered the church of Dr. Andrews, and became therein an active and zealous worker for her Master.

Her first appearance won the esteem and admiration of my father, although she was not so favorably impressed at first. The acquaintance, however, ripened into friendship, and finally into mutual affection. This continued until 1843, when they united the destinies and fortunes of their lives at the marriage altar. Now mated, they must needs have a home; and being of rural education and tastes, they naturally turned from the town. They first removed to a farm near Philadelphia, where, however, they were to remain but a short time. My grandfather taking ill, my father was called to the old home before the end of a year.

CHAPTER III.

THE DEATH OF MY GRANDPARENTS.

This sickness was, in the arrangement of Providence, to prove a sickness unto death. For more than sixty years William Smith had been a citizen of earth, but now a call to the higher life was to be heard. The old home-mansion of earth was to be exchanged for a new and better one in the skies. The whole life had been one grand tendency toward this. A pilgrim and a stranger here, he felt and knew that his *home* was in heaven. And now the end was reached; but the summons found him not unready, but waiting. Like a shock of corn fully ripe and in its season, he came down to the grave, while the spirit, like a buoyant bird, winged its way above. For very many years he had been a worthy member of the Presbyterian Church, and by blessed experience had learned to trust in the arm that could conquer every foe. Death, that wiliest and mightiest of all foes, was to be conquered also in its turn; and the conquest was to be most complete. Personally he had never before been brought down to Death's door, and, like many another, within hearing of the whelming Jordan. During life he had never had the doctor's care, nor even taken a portion of medicine until his final sickness. Yet the white messenger cast no shadow of fear over him as he advanced toward his couch, while to him the opening grave was as the cradle to a weary child. He proved that the soul could ride upon and above the waters, as did Noah within the ark. To him death was disarmed of its sting and the grave of its victory. If no other compensation can come of the Christian's trust, and as the reward for the heart's consecration to Jesus, than merely hopeful trust in death and triumph in that dreaded hour, who will say it is not enough that Christian labor has not adequate compensation? To the sacred bosom of the church-yard near by was given the precious dust of the holy man. Old neighbors and respected friends whispered with hushed tones and aching hearts, "The good man is dead." More rightly the sainted man was born again—born into a higher state and a holier life; not dead, but gone before; alive for evermore. The parting struggle was paralyzing to the hitherto vigorous form of my grandmother. Soon she, too, began to show unmistakable signs of early departure to the bed of death and the beautiful home beyond. She who had lived so long with him could not well live long without him. The heart was less joyous, and the gladsome glee of other days less common, while evidently the hold on life was fast loosening. A few months only elapsed, a measure of time less than that of a year, and the blessed twain were one again. Both had passed life's wilderness under God's law, and then had crossed the Jordan to the Canaan of rest. The family was now divided, and must henceforth scatter. The father was dead, and the maternal center was gone forever. The old homestead must pass from the family hands, although the happy scenes and sacred memories of early life could never be effaced. The sale transpired soon after the last death, and the proceeds of the home were divided among the children.

;

CHAPTER IV.

MY BIRTH.

My father bought with his allowance a small place of sixty acres, with a hotel property thereon, which had constituted a portion of my grandfather's estate. The hotel was now the home of my parents, my mother taking charge of the house and my father the general management of the farm. The hotel was of the old country fashion, and while affording entertainment for travelers it also had its bar for the sale of liquors. Rum, at that time, was almost the universal drink, and was common both to the field and the house. It was free alike to men and women, while the children were early allowed their portion. There were times when my mother had to dispense this common beverage, but ever, and from the first, with a feeling of disgust and earnest protest.

This necessity soon formed within my parents the resolution to leave the home that required a service so repugnant and distasteful. The hotel life was continued but for a year, a purchaser being found. Meantime, however, the light of day came to be my portion; and my presence, perhaps, lent an influence in hastening the change which had already been determined on. The hearts of my parents were never specially attached to this my natal home, so that to me the place of birth presents few of those pleasing attractions and poetic phases which gather around many such centers. There is no question but the soul is greatly advantaged throughout life if the first impressions made by home surroundings are of a happy nature. The heart can not but get helpful inspiration if, when led by its future retrospections back to its natal hour and home, the scene of life's beginning is one of beauty, loveliness, and comfort. But even in my birth I was favored more than some, and more indeed than He who as King of kings and Son of God came down to tabernacle in clay. For him there was no room in the inn, while for me the inn gave room; and hearts that dwelt therein gave welcome. The stable of the inn and the manger of the stable, these must answer for the Son of God. No room for the divine Babe in the inn, yet, praise the Lord, the world is now finding room for him; and blessed is the heart that can boast such a tenant as he.

CHAPTER V.

MY FATHER A MERCHANT AND A CHRISTIAN.

A country store, but a little distance away, was the next family center, and the scene of my earlier childhood. All of my father's means were put into this new enterprise; but, like many another, he managed his business affairs with too little prudence. Soon, by the credit system, his stock was greatly reduced, while the means for replenishing the fast-failing shelves were not speedily forthcoming. Demands, however, must be met, even if outstanding claims could not be controlled. One of those periodically recurring financial crises happening at that time, his doom was hastened, and at a great sacrifice my father sold his home and his stock. Broken up, without even a shelter they could call their own, they must seek a new home and a new center for honest and needed labor.

Whither should they look? Toward what point should they turn? If doubt and anxiety possessed them, many another has felt the pang of the same unpleasant experience. It was but natural that the heart of my mother, and indeed that of my father, should turn toward Doylestown, the scene and center of their earlier years, and of some and many of their sweetest associations. Heavier were their hearts as they retraced their steps than when they first went forth on their joint pilgrimage. They were now under a deep, dark cloud, but, as it proved at last, one which was but the Father's hand. Dark and angry it seemed; and yet from this very cloud were to come nourishing showers of grace. It is well at times that the sunshine be obscured, the way impeded, and the heart loaded with a cross of heaviness. So has it been with many in all the days of other years, and so will it be with many more in other days to come. Speedily, however, often the hour of deliverance will come, and we can say with David, "It is good for me that I have been afflicted." More than dark clouds covered the way of Moses and his hosts. Still, the way was ever opened finally, even though the sea had to be divided and its raging billows walled up on either hand. Nourishment could come in the arid plain, and the waste-howling wilderness could furnish a feast of bread and flesh. A cloud could cover them from their enemies, guide them in the way, and even illumine the darkness of the midnight.

Up to this time my father's heart had not been softened by the Spirit of grace. He had laid away the precious dust of father and mother into the narrow house of death; and he had felt keenly and bitterly his loss. Still, he had not made that blessed surrender indispensable to full and perfect preparation for a similar ordeal. The loss of property, severe adversity in outward circumstances, was to do for him what even the presence of death had not done. My mother had not forgotten the early vows of her religious home, and had probably at no time surrendered her hope in Christ. The thought of returning to Doylestown was refreshing to her, as it seemed to open anew the way to the sanctuary, and bring her nearer to the throne on high. In her sweet expectations she was not doomed to disappointment. The new home, though rented from another and not their own, was to prove, nevertheless, the sweetest and most sacred of any they had yet found. Dr. Andrews was still at the old church, and the home of this man of God was still open with its welcome to my mother and her own. Cordial friendship and real love were the offering of many hearts. These expressions had their effect upon my father, and the sanctuary became a place of frequent and regular resort. The ministrations of the desk were faithful, and they told upon his heart with melting and saving power. This, with a complete change in his associations, awakened within him a new interest, and led to a speedy consecration to the service

of his Master.   He confessed Christ, and with my
mother became a member of Dr. Andrews' church.
What though fortune had gone, and the home of
other days and the means of other years had been
lost?   Something more had been gained; yes,
even that which gold, with all its value, could not
purchase.

CHAPTER VI.

EARLY IMPRESSIONS; OR, CHILDHOOD MEMORIES.

The faithful pastor came frequently to our home; and under his holy ministrations, as I well recollect, the tears would course down my mother's cheeks, while her heart melted under the holy man's words of love. What wonder that my tender heart was touched, and especially as I, too, shared in the good man's blessing and in his kindly words! How strange that wise men will look no deeper into the volume of human nature—that the hearts of children are passed so long unnoticed and unfed! Have our teachers indeed forgotten the tenderness of their childhood hearts, and how wonderfully quickened they were under kindly notice and words of love? Those first impressions, as I sat beside my mother and listened to the minister's words, I have not lost them yet. Though the distance to the tomb be ever so far with me, nothing can efface them from my mind. The words are gone; no trace of the phraseology appears to memory; but the impression yet abides.

The altar of prayer was erected, and at it we gathered with rising sun and at decline of day.

Faithful was my father, and humble and holy were the words he said as he officiated before the altar of his home as a priest indeed. This was an early period in my life; but its lessons linger with freshness in my heart, as though they had their birth but in yesterday. What I owe to these impressions in this life I can never know, nor, had I an apostle's pen or an angel's tongue, could I hope to tell.

I was placed in the Sabbath-school at a very tender age, and soon became deeply interested therein. The simple lesson greatly excited my interest, while my heart was animated with a wonderful reverence for my teacher. I can see, as I look back upon those early days, that the teacher is possessed of a most wonderful power. While the child can not comprehend the broader phases and deeper significance of inspired truth, yet the heart is so tender that it will at once receive the simplest moral impressions. Not alone so; those impressions are absolutely ineffaceable. Forgetting, as some philosophers claim, is an impossibility. You may scratch ever so lightly upon the glass with the diamond, but you leave a mark that time can scarcely efface. You may forget the time when and the circumstances under which the line was graven, but the impression, nevertheless, is there, and must abide. So with the child, for his heart

is both impressible and retentive. The teacher
should present the truth in the simplest form, with
combined personal interest in the story and in the
heart receiving it. While I may not recall the
lessons I learned in those tender years, yet the impressions made by them are interwoven with my
life; and I must carry them down to my grave.
The child is not sufficiently credited either, perhaps, in the direction of merit or ability. He both
knows more than we imagine and deserves more
than he often receives. But while we admit his
capacity for understanding, it is even more important that we understand both the best method and
the shortest way of approach to his heart. I may
not tell the measure of love I had for my Sabbath-
school teacher; and it was but a response to a supposed manifestation of love from her heart. Love
properly addressed will reach the heart of any
child—reach, win, and hold him. It is the lever
by which the mother governs and by which God
himself moves and rules the world.

I did not simply attend the Sabbath-school; I
was also a child of the sanctuary. With my parents I mingled with the worshipers of God's
house; and in this I was certainly profited, if but
in the establishment of a habit which has proved
of life-long advantage. It is a wonderful mistake
that the child of to-day is so rarely seen in the

house of God among the worshipers! The Sabbath-school should not excuse him from the inner
sanctuary. The one should not be regarded as a
substitute for the other. However, I must confess
that my attendance was hardly a matter of choice,
but rather a result of compulsion. I could not
but feel that the sanctuary service was not for *me*,
and that the church of God was not *my* home.
There was something terrible to me in the sanctuary; it was a prison-house of restraint to my soul.
I felt almost afraid while there, and so longed to
get away. The benediction was my release, and I
heard its words with joy. Everything seemed so
solemn and sacred, I felt that the same spirit and
presence of death prevailed both within the church
and the grave-yard outside. The one I felt, somehow, to be but a preparation for the other. The
solemn tones of the organ seemed but the funeral
march from the pew and altar to the silence of the
grave. I wonder if these same icy chains yet bind
the hearts of our children; if to them the church
is the same *dreadful* place it used to be to me! If
so, no wonder they are such strangers to our pews,
and that they feel so strange within them. This
spirit of death-like solemnity pertains not of *right*
to God's house. The sanctuary should be a *home*
for the heart; and there should be ease and freedom
there, even for the children. The gloom should

be cast out, and the icy fetters need to be broken. The services of God's house should be adapted more fully than now to the wants of a simple, artless child. The voice of the pulpit should be more simple, and its spirit more familiar. The story of the cross, when told with simplicity to please and reach the child, will burn most deeply into the fleshly tablets of older hearts. Child-like simplicity is the want of the age; the one great want of the world.

The Sabbath as a *day*, I confess, was also a matter of dread to me. The school was almost the only oasis in the otherwise nearly barren desert. It was too much like a sick-room, where my voice, my feelings, and even my very breath needed to be suppressed. My little heart was in freezing fetters all the day,—fetters broken only by the morrow's rising sun. Sunday morning was the forging of fetters, while Monday morning was the bursting of chains. Somehow, Sunday to me was Christ's burial-day, and Monday broke to the world the joy of his resurrection. Sunday's rising sun seemed cold in hottest summer. The early hours seemed strange, while their revolutions were intolerably slow. I felt that I had no right to my own thoughts, and that my words were not good enough for the day. Even the indulgence of a smile seemed but a violence to the day. These impressions of

the Sabbath were such as my instructions and my
general surroundings were calculated to create.   It
was alike the lesson of home and that of the
church.   The words, spirit, and [teaching of our
minister seemed to throw a cloud over the day to
me.   Truly, we may not attach too much sanctity
to the Sabbath; but we should not enshroud it with
a mock solemnity, at once chilling to the heart and
repugnant to the feelings.   We should not bury
the day.   The Sabbath is for man, and not man
for the Sabbath.   It should be the most beautiful
and joyous day of all the seven; a day of welcome
to the weary; a day of gladness to the child.

CHAPTER VII.

MY SCHOOL-LIFE BEGINS.

And now opened another era in my career. I
was to be introduced to the day-school. My approach to it had been by the two blessed stations
of the sanctuary and the Sabbath-school. I was
about six years old when my father took me by
the hand and led me to the village school. I recollect well his saying to the teacher, "Sir, I wish
you to take good care of him, for he is a good boy."
Well, as I stood there holding my father's hand I
really thought I *was* a good boy. While my father in the goodness of his heart may have thought
so, too, I soon had painful reason for believing that
the teacher was of quite a different opinion. My
seat-mate proved to be an unfortunate companion
for me.

As I took my seat in the afternoon of one day,
toward the end of the first week, my teacher discovered a torn book, belonging to another scholar,
at my feet. I was charged with tearing it, while
my denial but enraged the teacher and made him
more positive of my guilt. I was placed for the
afternoon upon the dunce-block, with the dunce-
cap on my head and the torn book pinned to my

apron. Here was punishment greater than I, a child of six years, could bear. Well-nigh was my heart broken—broken, but not softened nor bettered. I was being punished for a crime of which I knew nothing. My punishment was a torture to my soul. What the wonder that this act roused the spirit of rebellion within me, and that it estranged and embittered my heart against that teacher? Surely I had met a tyrant in the start; but, like poor dog Tray, I was in bad company, and must suffer as the result.

I soon had another good reason for remembering the same poor dog, and giving him a full measure of my sympathy. On my way from school a battle was transpiring between two other boys. Naturally, I stopped to see the fun, as doubtless the teacher himself would have done had he been a child like me. While the fathers will talk of battles with so much zest, and praise the courage of the soldiery as a thing of highest value and merit, it is not strange that the children will try to imitate the heroism of their grandfathers, either by actual conflict or as interested witnesses of the exploit. In my case, however, I had heard but little in this line, and had seen less. But although the battle of the evening before was over, I was destined nevertheless to see the smoke of it on the next day. I was arraigned for participating in the fight, and accordingly punished with brutal severity. Here again, though actually innocent, I reaped the painful results of being in bad company. The natural and almost inevitable result of this second punishment was to make of me a bad boy, and to destroy all the love I had for the school. Coercion was now necessary, for the school had lost its charm. I looked in vain to the teacher for sympathy, while my parents unwisely saw little to condemn in his conduct. A mistake but far too common had been made; and the mere punishment was the mildest part of the disadvantage to me. The glory of my new life was under a cloud, and I was henceforth to grope my way in the dark. Sympathy and love I needed—these, with the kindly word. Instead, I felt the rod; and thereby my heart was stung and roused into rebellion and revenge. The youngest heart will quickly respond to the spirit of its master; and oh, what tender care should be taken in that spirit's birth. My father's determination to remove from Doylestown was hailed with living joy, for I felt that prison-bars were being left behind. A teacher's unguarded and maddened stroke had wounded my pride and blasted the glory of my village home. As I went forth I felt that Egypt was behind, and only Canaan before; but, like Israel, I soon learned that there was a wilderness ahead.

3

CHAPTER VIII.

THE NEW HOME.

My father was to become a farmer again, and I a farmer's son. The restraint of the village was to be exchanged for the freedom and salubrity of the country home and air. The removal was not far; but the change seemed great, and by none was appreciated more than by me. Experience in the life of farming was what I had never had, though born a farmer's son. The world seemed much greater and grander to me when the farm became my home; and even the heavens seemed bluer, brighter, and nearer than ever before. It appeared almost as though God created the country for himself, and really ruled therein, while the town was of man's creation, and had but man for its ruler. Everything seemed to say, "God has been here, and his hand hath formed and fashioned me." The woods, too, were so beautiful, and their green verdure so lovely, while the songsters of the wood seemed to sing all the day for me. And with what sweet melody they sung! Never had the music of the sanctuary appeared so much like praise or so touched my heart as the sweet carols of these free birds.

Our little farm-house, with its bright coat of fresh, yellow paint, was to me as a royal palace, while therein my father looked a king and my mother his beautiful queen. A little way to the eastward, deep down from the door of our home, was the old Turk mill-pond, which to me had the loveliness of the sea and the grandeur of the ocean. No painting of skillful artist could equal this. It was all beauty, such as the divine Artist only could form and fashion. The fish, as if made of silver and gold, were the sporting treasures of its silent depths, while its bosom was rippled by the proud water-fowl, whose motions were all elegance and grace. In summer-time, under golden sun and silver moon, the happy youth would plow the deep with oar and helm, beating and turning to the tune and time of merry song, while their merry hearts would send up to their cottage homes the tones of melody and the voice of glee. When old Boreas had stolen down from the north and locked the silver ripples in cold and silent sleep, and built his proud highway from shore to shore, then young men and maidens would share in the skater's skill and the coaster's sport until the silence of the forest and the illumination of the hills proclaimed the hour of rest for all.

The Big Neshaminy, winding among the hills
in the neighborhood, and crooking itself like a
serpent, as if disputing with rugged nature the
right of personal being, was one of the most pict-
uresque streams of any country. From its elevat-
ed origin and its large volume it afforded power
for numerous mills, so that besides nourishing the
soil which produced our grain, it provided also the
strength which ground the corn for our bread.
From either side of this stream bold bluffs arose,
as if Nature, in her stalwart sons, would look down
with an eye of scrutiny upon this intruder while
hastening on his winding way. On the inside of
the elbow of the Big Neshaminy, surmounting
one of these lordly bluffs, was an old stone building, which served in its room below for the week-
day school, and in its room above for the services
of the Sabbath-school and church. What a grand
place was this for the education of the sons and
daughters of Nature's noblemen. With the eye
upon the romantic beauty of surrounding nature,
how could the heart fail to catch an inspiration
which would make it gigantic in its strength?
With the roar of the rumbling stream below, into
which, from the window above, one could plunge
a stone even without the aid of a David's sling,
and with the almost ceaseless voice of the old mill
in the vale below, why should not the heart of a

school-boy be glad, and his voice defiantly bold? If here was not a field of freedom for the liberated heart, where, in all the world, could such a place be found? On this winding stream I first tried my skill as a traveler on skates; and with many falls and serious bumps I took my first lessons as a star-gazer. Coasting from the bold bluff above to the frozen stream below, with dizzy gyrations on skates and the building of old snow-forts, was sport enough for winter, while with the native charms of summer came the pleasures of fishing, boating, and bathing.

But all of the attractions of those days did not center in the room below. There was a school above of blessed memory. Dr. Andrews conducted the service above as preacher, and noble men and women from the country about served as teachers. To me the doctor's preaching seemed very different from that which he gave in town, and really better withal. And then, in his manner he seemed more like a man and a father. While we could get nearer to him, his talk, also, was more direct and familiar. I could greatly enjoy his preaching here, while the charm of the Sabbath-school was wonderfully increased.

CHAPTER IX.

THE CRADLE AND THE GRAVE.

While these general changes were transpiring without, others, also, were going on within our home. I was no longer the only child. God gave me a brother for my companionship; and a darling brother he was to me. Taught to believe that he came down from God, he certainly *seemed* the gift of Heaven to me. If not an angel in all respects, to me he seemed even more than an angel. For the company of no one of that thriving retinue would I have given him.

"Our baby," and "my brother," were boastful words with me, and their possibility afforded occasion for real pride. And then a baby sister came to us—a gray-eyed baby sister; the prettiest babe in the world, I thought. And she was to me as the treasure of a king. How rich now was I with a brother, and a sister too! But the brother was not long to stay. He was only to begin here a life that should never end. *From* above, he was to go back again too soon. Almost with his birth the angels had begun to arrange for him a home on

high with them. Soon I was to know by a sad
experience what that was of which my parents
had so often talked, and of which our minister had
so often warned. I was to know the dreadful
meaning of *death*, and to see and feel its presence
in my own home.

Three years only had the dear boy lived with us
in the old farm-home. But oh, how he had added
to the music of that home during the few brief
years of his stay. "Too good for earth," some
said he was, and others, "Too bright and active
for a lengthy stay below." Not too good, I felt
very sure, for none are too good for earth who belong to the mortal form. Angels have come down
into the human form, and for the few brief hours
of a day have tarried with the sons of men, while
He who was infinitely more than the angels, even
God's own blessed Son, had dwelt with men for
many years. The mind of my dear brother, however, was too active for the frail, feeble form, and
under its energy the body withered and the soul
burst its bars and fled. From memory of the recitations of others he would repeat or answer whole
chapters of the catechism. Though he lived not
long, he must have learned many lessons that gave
a familiar air to the home and life on high as he
rose up from earth and entered into the holy city.
When there, I fancy he at once felt himself at

home. I well remember how, as he sat on my father's knee, he listened to the story of the Savior's life and death. Told once, he would ask that it might be told again.

One day the fever came, and his cheeks were all aflush with flame. Oh, he seemed so sick, and suffered so much. How I studied the face of my mother as she bowed over the form of my brother! Thus I sought to read her thoughts and know how the darling was. He sometimes asked for me; but I felt that the icy king had hold of his hand, and for fear of the monster I dreaded to approach my brother's bed. From his bed I shrunk, and forth from the room I sought freedom and safety. The doctor's care and my mother's anxious watching seemed to avail nothing against the fever's fire. Oh, how I prayed that God would not call him back again to his native home. But this praying availed me nothing, for death soon came. His lips grew cold, and bore no kiss for me; his eyes were sealed, and sent no smile to me. He was *dead;* and now, in all the world, I had no brother!

Dr. Andrews came, and by my mother's side spoke words which, though they gave relief to the heart, yet added freely to the stream of scalding tears. Prayer was more solemn than ever, and the light of home seemed forever withdrawn. Then came the coffin-case to cradle my brother's form. Oh, it seemed to me that he should never be taken from his bed of down. To transfer his little body therefrom to the cold, dismal coffin seemed a final act of cruelty. And now the funeral-day was come, and he was to be borne forth to the bed of death, in the lonely burial-ground. The place from which I shrunk, and toward which I hardly dared to turn my gaze or thought, was to become the resting-place of him I loved so tenderly. From *my* bed he was to go forth and lie down in the bed of death *alone*. The man of God, with tender emotion, conducted the solemn service, and then, for the last time, the coffin-lid was raised for the gaze of friends. Oh, my heart seemed breaking within me as I looked into that face for the last time. Never again, in all this life, was I to see him more. The last look was taken amid the sobbings of melted, broken hearts, and we turned away forever. The lid was sealed, the tiny body borne forth, the procession formed, and toward the old church-yard we slowly moved. Oh, what a solemn march! Even the birds seemed to sing as if death was in their thought, and their cadences but added to the gloom of the hour. We lowered him into the dark chamber of the grave, with the *dead* as his only companions. It seemed to me there ought to be *one* window in that grave, through which we might look down on him. But he had

the watch of angels, and God would not forget his
dust. The homeward ride was one of added gloom.
Going forth, *he* was one with us; homeward, we
were alone! The old home appeared no longer
home, and the shadows of coming night seemed
but the return of the wings of death.

CHAPTER X.

A PECULIAR PEOPLE.

The care of the farm upon which we lived, together with the sorrow consequent upon the death of my brother, told severely upon my father, while the increased care of my mother from God's gift to us of another child, a dear blue-eyed sister, determined my folks to remove to a small place in another neighborhood, a few miles away. I confess to much reluctance on my own part in leaving forever a home which had been so pleasant, and which had become so sacred withal by the birth of two sisters and the death of my only brother. And then the removal would take us farther from his grave, and make our visit thereto an infrequent occurrence. There was much to give up; and I found that I had by no means the same feeling as that with which I left the village of Doylestown.

The new home to me was not one of real interest or special beauty. It had not the romantic surroundings of that from which we came; but the general feeling to me was one of gloom and

unhome-likeness.' The neighborhood did not afford me the same advantages in companionship or
facilities for schooling, while the old Sabbath-school
in the stone house on the bluff, by the winding
Big Neshaminy, was never in its like to be found
again. Still, with the disadvantages there were
many advantages in the removal. If I lost in my
social companionship, I gained beyond question in
my religious surroundings. I had, up to this time,
been trained exclusively under Puritanical and
Presbyterian influences; and in the religious world
I knew nothing else than that cold, severe type of
theology and training. My nature longed for the
warmer aspects of religion, and for a nearer and
more social approach to the fountain of spiritual
life. I had lived thus far too largely on the north
side of life, so to speak, and now I was to pass
around to the sunnier south and warm the other
side of my nature. My teaching had been too
much from an intellectual stand-point, and withal
too formal. It had been a good foundation to
build upon; but now that the walls of the temple
were to go up higher, there needed to be a blend-
ing of softer materials with the cold and solid
granite.

To the eastward of a large tract of tall, gnarled
oaks, in a small opening, stood a plain-looking but
tasteful church-house, of small dimensions. There

was a small open yard in front, while in the rear
was a large space consecrated to the burial of the
neighborhood dead. This was the only church
within a circuit of several miles. It was owned
by the Tunkers—more familiarly known as Dunk-
ards. My mother had often spoken to me of
their peculiar methods of worship and their baptism. I had often witnessed this ceremony in the
old church at Doylestown; and at the sacred font,
it was said, I had been baptized, and my brothers
and sisters afterward. What other form of baptism could there be? My curiosity was at fever
heat, and I longed for an opportunity to witness
the rite in the new form of this singular people.

Soon after our removal, and at the very first
meeting held by this people thereafter, an opportunity offered. Baptism was announced, and I had
the consent of my parents to attend. Besides baptism, I was to be the witness of other and even
stranger things. At the church the men saluted
each other not alone with extended hand, but with
cordial kiss, displaying a familiarity and a degree
of fellowship which I supposed wholly unknown
among men. My astonishment increased as I entered the church. Surely it was entirely unlike the
only church I knew. No organ sent forth its peals
of solemn music, while no carpet covered the floor
or cushions the pews of the house. The men, with

long, flowing locks, and hair parted in the middle, were seated by themselves on one side of the church, while the women, seated by themselves, were ranged on the other side. Their heads were divested of bonnets, while they were crowned with caps of delicate whiteness. The man of God who was to minister at the altar was the model of a farmer of the plainest type. The song was no artistic display of choral band, but a spontaneous outburst of praise from tongues and hearts all attuned by the Spirit of God. Such music I had never heard. They sung with the freedom of the warblers of the wilderness, and, as if like them, their voices were addressed to God. And then when the minister said, "*Let us pray,*" the congregation arose but to fall upon their knees before the throne. It was a sight to see, and the vision entranced my soul. I felt that God was there, and that the people were indeed his children.

It did seem to me that I had never witnessed worship before; and probably by no display that I had ever beheld had I been carried so completely into the presence of my Master. The discourse which followed was expository, covering nearly an entire chapter, and to me was intensely interesting. Dismissed, the congregation repaired to the stream near by for baptism. I was in a good frame of mind to witness the ceremony, and had

a commanding position on a bridge near the scene.
The candidate once within the stream, he kneeled,
and certain questions being asked and answered, a
blessing was invoked upon the new disciple. The
candidate was now immersed in water, face foremost, three times, once each in the three blessed
names of Father, Son, and Holy Ghost. Arising,
the candidate was led forth and greeted in the most
cordial and affectionate manner, receiving the extended hand and the kiss of welcome. As I went
to my home I felt that indeed I had witnessed
strange things that day. With wonderful anima-
tion I related my experience to my parents, who
received my story with seeming indifference, I
thought

In the evening I was permitted to worship with
this people again. The center of the house I found
vacated of the pews, and in their stead a table
spread with a frugal meal. Following a brief sermon, they partook of this, with water only for
their drink. Preceding this was the ceremony of
feet-washing, and the holy communion followed.
I was much pleased with what I saw, and felt that
in all these things the heart had a place. I had
never seen such social, fraternal, and affectionate
manifestations before, nor such living signs of real
Christian brotherhood. Whatever their theology
might be, I loved the people for what they appear-

to be. I felt at home, longed to go again, and
thought I should be most happy if I could but fully
share in their work of worship. This experience
inclined me to think and talk a great deal about
religious matters. I felt that this people were possessed of a feeling and an experience with which I
was wholly unacquainted. I was uneasy, and felt
that I should do something for my own safety. I
had ever reverenced the church, but now I was
really in love with and felt that I should be a
member of it. In the anxiety of my heart I naturally approached my mother. She assured me
that virtually I was a church-member, and would
soon be old enough for confirmation as a member.
But my love for the Doylestown church was growing cold, and I was only too glad that my folks so
readily found excuses for remaining away. Since
witnessing the worship of the Tunkers, that at
Doylestown seemed cold and more formal than ever. The preaching of the Tunker Church was
only occasional, and I consequently saw less of
their worship than I desired.

CHAPTER XI.

THE MODEL TEACHER.

Their Sabbath-school was held regularly, how-ever, and therein I was soon a regular and an in-terested attendant. Now, instead of coming to the catechism, I found myself approaching more di-rectly than ever the Word itself. I was being brought into cordial contact, also, with a form of life for which I thirsted. I was to find friends that could sympathize with my want, and direct me in my gropings after truth. What wonder, then, that my soul warmed with a new love, even toward men that seemed so strange. These rough men were to write impressions on my heart that were to largely change my ways, and even mold my life. I began to rejoice in the change we had made.

Heretofore my Sabbath-school teachers had been ladies, and I had felt a special freedom in approach-ing them. The tenderness of motherhood and sister-hood seems best suited to the wants of the child-like heart; and doubtless our most effective and acceptable teachers are ladies. In this direction,

4

however, I was to have a new experience; I was
to have my first gentleman teacher.   I was to learn
that a man's heart had not simply an austere and
commanding phase, but a tender and affectionate
side.   A gentleman of about forty years, with dark
eyes and curly black hair, a Mr. C., was to expound
the holy word to my class, and break the bread
of life to my soul.   I found, rather to my surprise,
that I could freely approach him; and I discovered for him at once in my heart a cordial regard
and a hearty reverence.   He showed from the start
a double interest—first, in the lesson expounded,
and then in the student taught.   He felt after the
hearts of his scholars, and sought to impress them
with a conviction of the presence of his Master,
and to infuse into their hearts the spirit of that
Master.   To save as well as teach, he accepted as
his obligation; and he made this thought specially
manifest to each of us.   From the depth of his
concern, I began to feel that I was really in danger.
So far in life it had appeared to me that I was in
Sabbath-school simply and only for real, solid
work, and that this school of the Sabbath differed
from the week-day school only in the nature of
that work.   The school had failed to impress me
with a sense of personal concern or want.   I had
failed until now to see myself a sinner, or to learn
even that others thought of me as a sinner or one

in need of helping Heaven. While heretofore love
had been exhibited, now there was manifest a tender solicitude that seemed strange, and something
which I could not understand. Why should this
strange, strong man take an interest in me which
other teachers heretofore, and even my own father
and mother, had not? I began to feel myself a
patient, and that I could accept my teacher as the
needed physician of my soul. He talked of religion as though he loved it and was familiar with it.
This seemed strange to me, for in the simplicity of
my heart I had concluded that men did not like to
speak of religion, nor even of the name of its
great Teacher. If mentioned, it was certainly generally in the spirit of apology, if not in its language. I had learned heartily to pity a person
when under the necessity of such a labor. I regarded this familiar mention of religious matters
as the work alone of ministers. I could not but
think of them as wonderfully courageous men, to
speak so boldly to others of their Master. But
now, how different! It no longer seemed to me
as something far-fetched and foreign to the soil of
the soul, but rather as a genial life, bubbling up from
this man's heart. Religion had never seemed so
beautiful before as I saw it in the general habits,
manners, words, and spirit of this Mr. C. Evidently his work was not simply that of a formal

teacher, nor even primarily this. He appeared more to me as a servant of God, one whose business it was to win disciples for the Master.

Nor were the school-room and the Sabbath-day the only place and time for his employment. Every day and every place seemed the same to him. I was made to feel that I was his scholar seven days in the week, instead of one, and on the street and in the field as well as in his class. He would often talk personally to me of religion, outside of the class and the room, and even take me to his home and table. What a wonderful impression this familiar intercourse and this courteous attention had on me! I felt myself both honored and loved. And then when the evening for prayer-meeting came he would often call for me at my home, and ask my company to the house of God. What wonder that my heart was touched, and that I formed an interest in this man that amounted even to love itself. However, I was not yet to yield to this blessed persuasion of a holy life. Why I did not I shall never understand, and shall never cease to regret that I did not

CHAPTER XII.

COUNTERACTING INFLUENCES.

Unfortunately for me, there were other and counteracting influences at work. Of these, in a few words, I must speak. My immediate companions were boys of rather rough habits, though of genial and cordial natures. With them the habits of chewing, smoking, and profanity were heartily indulged and fixed. I eagerly shrunk from all of these, and regarded them as trifling, degrading, and even brutish. I felt that I would give anything to dissuade my friends from pursuing them. In this, however, I did not succeed; but as their ways became familiar I felt less objection to them, took less notice of them, and was perceptibly influenced by them. The habit of smoking I accepted as something somehow manly, but secretly practiced it for fear of my parents. Chewing disgusted me, while profanity shocked me, and neither habit could I consent for a moment to adopt.

I did adopt some foolish by-words, although profane words never had up to this time, I am proud to say, passed my lips. These coarse words, however, blunted my conscience gradually, and led me to listen somewhat composedly to bolder words. Indeed, this partial compromise was but an encouragement to actual profanity in my mates. I have been wonderfully astonished. since in my life, and was often in the days of my boyhood, to hear even simplest by-words and foolish, nonsensical talk from persons of holy profession. It ever seemed to me as a cowardly approach to the worst habits of boldly wicked men. Such coarse and foolish talk ever lowered men of holy professions in my mind; and no such persons could possibly have reached me from a religious stand-point under any circumstances. Christian men do not sufficiently realize how watchful and critical children and youth are, especially toward those whom, by profession, they are led to regard as holy. A vast multitude of tender youth are driven from virtue's center by unseemly conduct in professing men.

Up to this period of my life I had never been allowed to go beyond the sacred precincts of home after the shades of night had fallen, except on errands or to centers of social and religious interest. The country store was near by, and it was the resort of many lounging, idling men and boys, in whose foolish talk there was much to disgust, and yet some things to charm. My mates were wont

to gather here, and I gladly formed excuses to be-
take myself to the same resort,—at first with
a feeling of hesitation and shame, and afterward
with boldness and confidence. This habit had upon me, as I could see at that time, and as since
I have most painfully seen, a really pernicious effect. Many habits are learned from the rough talk
of such a resort that will be accepted, and which
often are not rejected until sorrow, shame, and ruin
are reaped in consequence. The home fireside for
the evening hour is the safest place for the forming
mind of the child; and not until the habits of
youth are well fixed may they safely go forth from
these God-created centers. Home should be made
more attractive than what it usually is. Too often
the child finds himself in the way, or he feels
chained down by a restraint that makes him
long for freedom and relief. There is not familiarity enough between parents and their children.
The idea that a child may approach the parents of
a mate more freely than he can his own is a
most terrible mistake. Yet this is too often and
generally the case. No wonder, then, that young
people seek release from home in the familiar spirit
and expressions that can not be found at home.
This absence from home and resort to the country
store operated severely against the influence of my
teacher, and almost entirely counteracted the good

man's work for a hold upon my heart. I began
to desire that he should somewhat loosen his hold
on me; and with increasing interest in my bold
companions I felt less interest in him.

CHAPTER XIII.

A NEW BROTHER AND A NEW HOME.

Here in this home I was blessed again with the gift of a baby brother. Our Willie was not to take entirely the place of Ross, the darling brother we had lain away in the old church-yard at Doylestown, but he was to share with me in possessing and loving him. I was happy again in the sweet thought that once more I had a brother; and yet from the first I lived in constant fear that, like my brother Ross, Willie, too, might die. This dear brother, however, was to be spared for a good number of years, and was to become to me a brother indeed—a dear companion of unspeakable value. He will have a large place, as in every way he deserved, in the future pages of this book.

Meantime another removal was determined on Once more we were to go forth as pilgrims; and from a new center I was to experience changes and form associations that would tell deeply upon the future of my being and my work. A neighborhood of many blessed associations was to be left, and perhaps before the saving impressions

received were entirely neutralized. We were to
return toward the old Neshaminy home. Spring-
time had come, and the loveliness of nature seemed
almost at its best. It was a good time to change,
when the birds were returning and when the heavens and the earth were both opening into the grandeur and glory of a new and happier life. In the
improvement of the natural surroundings the
change was one of great interest, and most acceptable to me. A lovelier spot in all that country, if
indeed in any other, could hardly be found. Its
beauty even surpassed that of the home on the
hill-side, in the old yellow farm-house. The Big
Neshaminy was to be my welcome companion
again. Its serpentine form I was to trace, its fish
I was to bait and ensnare, while its old, bold roar
was to gladden my heart and quicken my spirits
again. It was but a few moments' walk from the
old stone house which was to become our home,
and its merry music was ever within reach of my
listening ear. A large, beautiful mill-pond was
near by, and stretched out within the easy scope
of vision and of call. It spread out its placid
waters to the west and south as one grand scene
of loveliness and beauty. Toward the north-east
the Pennsylvania Railroad passed our home from
the south-west, separated only by a ten-acre field.
The daily dashing of the train and the frequent

sounding of the voice of steam were welcome com-
panious by day and by night, and never could I
weary of the sight of the one or the sound of the other. The station of New Brittain was within a few
minutes' walk of our door, and ever a center of
living interest to me. Of these railroad scenes the
busy world can never grow weary, and those most
engaged can stop for a moment's gaze.

Standing by the station one day, I noticed the peculiar motions of a stranger as he cautiously alighted
and kept careful hold of a boyish hand. In another
moment my heart was welling over with sympathy for him. I was looking for the first time in
my life upon one who was blind. The lovely vision of nature and of life has passed forever from
his gaze. Oh, how my heart melted in pity for
him. How I longed to give him for a time the
sight of my own eyes, or at least the light and the
luster of one. I am sure that in that moment I
would gladly have shared the glory of vision with
him. While I thought how terrible must be his
gloom, and how desponding must be his heart, it
did not in the most remote manner enter my mind
that I ever should be blind, and that I, like him,
should ever seek the friendly hand to guide my
weary feet. How blessed that we know so little
of the future; that its dark ways are so obscured, or rather illumed, with bright visions which

are never to know a living reality. What a load
my heart would have carried from that hour had
God commissioned that man to say to me, "Thou
shalt in early years to come be blind thyself, and,
like me, shall seek the guidance of another." A
gracious Providence spared me the prophecy, and
kept my soul in ignorance of the vision and the
reality. *I was to become blind!* Dreadful truth!
But God showed me his tender mercy in withholding from my thought the solemn fact of that perpetual night into which my sun of day was soon
to sink. We know enough of the future, and we
do well to wisely improve the precious present.
We know not what a day may bring forth. The
future shall embosom both the sunshine and the
shadow; and with the tranquil sky shall appear
the angry storm. It is much to know, however,
that wherever we go God shall lead our feet and
direct our way if we but consent. This blind gentleman was Professor Dyer, from Philadelphia.
He had come to our village for a series of concerts,
and his home was to be at our house. By this
means I became well acquainted with him, only,
however, to realize an increased sympathy for his
hapless condition.

In the little village surrounding the station, as
a grandly conspicuous object, was a large stone
meeting-house, owned by, and wherein worshiped,

a Baptist congregation. Connected with the house
was an immense—or so it seemed then to me—
burial-ground. The congregation, and indeed the
country about for a circuit of many miles, here
gathered and buried their precious dead. The old
white tomb-stones were at first a solemn scene as
I gazed upon them from my home; but after a
time, with their solemnity there seemed to com-
mingle a real beauty. I cared not for the near approach, but as I withdrew to a distance there was
a charm in their appearance. Many a soul has
been uplifted by the solemn and ghost-like mon-
uments of the sleeping dead, whose names and
deeds they commemorate. Though they seem to
keep watch over sacred dust, yet upward do they
lift the finger of solemn silence to the soul of the
passer-by. The church-house was large, and would
accommodate the entire surrounding neighborhood.
It was the only church of the village, and was
destined to become a center of special interest to
me. Against the Baptists I had a feeling of special
prejudice; and had I been called to express their
characteristics, I should have used but two words
—exclusive and selfish. But I was getting out of
the narrow circle of a single creed, and was fast
learning that the world was exceeding broad, and
that in religion, as in nature, there was a wonderful and beautiful variety. Morever, I was coming

into a field of observation, study, and real life that was to entirely change many narrow notions and crude convictions of my other days

I also was to be able to hear preaching every Sabbath, and even twice a day. The first Sabbath after our arrival at our new home I went to hear Rev. Mr. Wheat, the minister in charge. Well do I remember both the text, and the impression produced by the sermon: " A bruised reed shall he not break, and the smoking flax shall he not quench." From this text he preached as I thought I had never heard preaching before. I felt as though his piercing black eyes were fixed on me, and that they penetrated to the inmost depths of my secret soul. I actually shrunk behind the pillars that supported the gallery, gratified, too, for the protection they afforded me. I certainly had never heard a sermon that seemed so intended for and so directly aimed at me. Nevertheless, I was deeply interested, and much enjoyed the service. There was a warmth in his manners and a directness in his words that impressed me deeply, and carried conviction to my heart. I thought much of that sermon in my homeward walk, and only as I sunk into sleep could I cease the reflections awakened by it. I looked forward to the coming Sabbath with great interest, and longed for the tardy revolutions of the week to pass and be gone.

CHAPTER XIV.

ALMOST PERSUADED.

At the morning Sabbath-school I gathered with the rest, though a stranger to all. However, I felt at home from the general friendliness of the people, the peculiar sanctity of the place, and the kindly disposition of the scholars. I was placed in a Bible-class of boys of my own age, under the care of a Mr. S., a genial, middle-aged gentleman. I became deeply interested at once in this gentleman, from his cordial expressions of friendly feeling and from his special interest in my personal case religiously. The Bible alone was the text-book of our class; and most thoroughly did we study it. In a most friendly manner would the teacher address each scholar personally, and by a singular and yet pleasing method draw from us a sort of review of our general thought and conduct for the week. His one anxiety seemed to be that his scholars should become Christians. Nor was this anxiety expressed in a bold and objectionable manner. He offended none by this anxious look

into our life, but gained steadily on the affection
of all. On the street he would ever recognize us,
give us his cordial word, and perhaps inquire how
we were spending our time, and if we took time
for prayer.

We knew that we were the subjects of his daily
prayer, according to his own assurance; and this
very fact, as it came to our minds by day and by
night, strongly impressed us. His spirit was fatherly and cordial; and never did a teacher, I am
sure, have a stronger hold on the affection of his
scholars. The superintendent, Mr. S., was also a
gentlemanly Christian, and displayed, as I now
see and remember, a wonderful interest, both in the
general school and the particular scholars of the
school. If he did occupy a higher place, yet he
was about as near and dear to us as were our teachers. I had a feeling, which I am now sure was
generally shared by the scholars, that he had a special, personal interest in each, and that each largely
shared his friendship and love. On the street, by
the brook or railway, wherever, indeed, we met
him, he had for us a kindly look and a friendly
word. Many a time he has taken a seat by my
side and discoursed to me, in a simple and familiar
manner, about the sublimity of nature, the beauties of revelation, and the well-being of my soul.
He would call at my home, as would also my teach-

er, and thereby seek to interest both myself and
my father's family in the work of the Sabbath-
school. The congregation of this church, too, had
a great many personal workers; and by their kindly approaches I was made to feel a new interest in
myself, and a new interest also in the world in
which I lived. A special effort was made to bring
the scholars of the school into the prayer-meetings; and it was no unusual thing for the teachers
to call for their scholars and conduct them to the
house of the Lord.

Adjacent to the meeting-house, and within the
church-yard, was an artificial pool, fed from a bubbling spring high up on the hill-side. This pool
was used for baptismal services generally, although
at some seasons of the year they would retire to
the Big Neshaminy, and under the pleasant shade
of the giant sycamores perform the baptismal rite.
I had witnessed baptism in two different forms before coming to this place, and it seemed very
strange to me that still another form for the same
rite could be in use. I had now an opportunity to
witness the rite in a third form. Some half dozen
candidates were to be immersed, and I certainly
was among the most interested of the spectators.
As they went under the water I could not but feel
that they were indeed buried in the likeness of the
Savior's burial; and as they came up from the bap-

5

tismal grave it impressively reminded me of the
Savior's resurrection. It did not seem to me that
there was too much water for the baptismal rite;
nor could I see any reason why, when once immersed, they should be buried twice more. There
was to me a remarkable beauty and simplicity in the
form; and I felt much surprised that all the world
could not see it as correct, and adopt it as such.
Young as I was, the witnessing of this act had
made me a convert to the mode. These baptisms
were of common occurrence, and to me they ever
seemed beautifully solemn and strangely impressive.
I ever longed for their recurrence, and often wished that I was among the candidates.

By a strange and terrible providence the ship
fever, as it was called, was introduced into our
neighborhood, and within a few days an entire
family of some ten persons were prostrated by it,
and swept into the grave. Besides, several other
families suffered severely; so that in the course of
two weeks twenty or more persons were hurried
into eternity. It is not strange that a wonderful
solemnity settled upon the church and the people
generally. I was certainly never so wrought upon
in my life. To witness these burials, so near to
my own door and with such alarming frequency,
led me to realize the near approach of time and
eternity, and to feel the importance of an early

and immediate preparation. The minister became more earnest, the prayer-meetings more solemn, and soon a revival state existed in the church and neighborhood. Several of my mates confessed Christ at the altar of prayer and in the waters of baptism. The appeals of the faithful minister touched and moved me greatly. He would come down the aisle and talk personally with us; and often he would kneel by our side and pray directly and most fervently for us. Many followed him to the altar and accepted the gracious offers of salvation. How happy I thought them, and how in my heart I envied them. I would have advised the entire audience to go and join them at the altar in their confession. They were but doing what I longed to do; they had come to a determination which for myself I was seeking to establish. I felt that the decision was not with me; it was not in my power. The minister, superintendent, teacher, members, and even my own mates, were personally appealing to and entreating with me. They were but acting in perfect harmony with my own feelings. Wishing every one else to go, of course I wished and longed myself to go. Personal appeal was not necessary in my case; but permission was. To solve the problem I naturally turned to my parents, and yet with more than half a fear that I should not have their consent. They were

Presbyterians, and could not willingly consent that their child should become a Baptist.
They failed to fan the spark of desire within me
into a flame of devotion. I would have given a
world, as I felt, could they have heartily approved
the revival work and consented to my share in the
same. A single word of encouragement in that
direction would have sent me to the altar and
numbered me then and there among the followers
of the Lamb of God. As much as I longed to go,
I could not against their wish and without their
consent. I felt that I should enter, and that henceforth my study should be with the ministry in view.

The theological school was almost constantly a
vision before me, and seemed a step in the road
that God would have me travel. My parents were
honest in their convictions and prejudices beyond
question, and while withholding their encouragement felt conscientious and justifiable. I have
never indulged in any reflections against them, and
have never felt a particle less of love for them for
the course they pursued. However, could they
have shared my feelings and seconded my desire, it
would have proved the greatest possible good to
them and ten thousand blessings for me.

Parents should watch for the first signs of the
religious life, and give every possible encouragement to its development. Salvation may hardly

come at too tender an age, while the child-convert is quite as sure to honor his profession and prove a good, steadfast soldier as converts of maturer age and experience. Consecration at the altar will do more than all things else to fix the habits of the child and to save him from the withering temptations of life. If in any period of life he needs the helps of religion, it is during the tempestuous days of youth. Carry him up to manhood within daily sight of the altar, and within daily hearing of the voice of prayer before the altar, and his safety is almost assured. Of the criminals of London it has been ascertained that ninety-seven per cent became what they were before reaching the age of twenty-one years. Thus, it is seen, habits of criminality are formed in youth, the very season, too, when the heart is most easily reached for Jesus. If Satan seeks pupils for his school and servants for his work among those of tender years, surely the church should not pass the *lambs* while seeking disciples for its Master.

CHAPTER XV.

CITY COMPANY.

The romantic nature of our present situation, together with the roominess of our home accommodations, determined my parents to advertise for summer boarders from the city.   Soon applications for entertainment came in from a large number of parties; and during the summer months we accommodated an average of twenty or more ladies and gentlemen.   They were generally from the higher social stations of life, and were most excellent company, as one may imagine.   I soon became deeply interested in them, and was, unconsciously to myself, wonderfully influenced by them. How far they shaped my future I could hardly tell.   I was general errand-boy for the company, and was pilot, usually, for their boating, fishing, riding, and rambling excursions.   As a rule they were not of a spiritual class, and did not seek the country air and sports for the mere cultivation of the spiritual.   With them they brought their light and trashy literature, also cards, and other games. Their literature I read, their games I saw, and their influence upon me may better be imagined

than told. Seeds were sown that yielded, as we
shall see, bitter fruitage for many years. I culti-
vated the habit of foolish reading, of course,
and soon the company failed to furnish all that I
required. In search of novels, I ransacked the
neighborhood, and for their purchase I spent the
few dimes I earned. Tales of ocean life and bor-
der reminiscences were my delight; and during the
long hours of many a night have I read and spec-
ulated over the pages of fancy fiction. Home began to lose its charms, and I wished myself an
adventurer among the homeless sons of men.

Amid almost perfect happiness I looked forth
into the deep, dark world for what it had not to
give. A mother's daily love, a father's kindly
words, the sweet, innocent affection of a baby
brother and darling sisters—all of these, combined
with many another blessing, could not lend charms
enough to the life I wished to lead. Like many
another foolish youth, I would go forth from all
alone. I would be a wanderer among men, an adventurer among heroes; and I would have both
fortune and renown as my reward. I ventured to
unfold my dreams to my mother, and make known
to her my wish; but no consent was given to my
crazy purposes. Then, like a hero, I resolved to
go, even if against the wishes and pleadings of
those who loved me best. Had not others gone

forth under the protecting shades of night alone? So, too, could I. If I could be free in no other way, I would run away. The seeds of fiction were ripening in my heart, and I was reaching forth the sickle to reap the grain.

My school advantages had now become better than ever before. Excellent teachers and a good system of instruction were afforded me, while my own age and strength were all to my advantage in my study. I could now see out somewhat far into the earthly life; could understand somewhat better the nature and obligations of man's earthly career, and had risen to a degree beyond many of the trifling and foolish habits of boyhood. Could I have put my attention upon my studies, I should have made rapid progress, as I needed to. But I had lost nearly all interest in the work of the school. Other matters were now distracting my mind and claiming my attention. I did not feel at home in the school-room; I wished to be outside, and away from its duties. I felt, young as I was, that I was needed elsewhere; and I would be free, that I might go. I was a student simply from compulsion, and felt little interest longer in the perfect lesson. I was neither ambitious to excel nor ashamed of my failure to master my studies and equal the proficiency of my mates.

The church was no longer the favorite resort that it had been in other days. The services made little impression upon my mind, and attendance upon them was really not for the lessons they inculcated. My heart was no longer susceptible to those hallowed influences which had once aroused it, while the man of God, who ministered at the altar, was not now possessed of the wonderful power over me he once wielded. I dreaded now, also, to attend the sanctuary, while the Sabbath-school had lost nearly all of its charms. The lesson did not impress me as formerly, nor did I wish it should. Other lessons interested me more. The servants of the Master I cared not to meet, and whenever possible I avoided their presence. If on the opposite side of the street from me, I felt best satisfied, and would often give myself the benefit of that degree of distance.

Spring had come again, and Nature once more was crowning herself in lovely attire. Still, its beauties did not attract me as formerly. I was losing my relish for even the lovely scenes of the Big Neshaminy valley. I felt sure that nature was as lovely everywhere, and that the world had many charms of which I had not even dreamed. Why should I not see them and share in the richness of their glory? Why should I remain a prisoner forever within my father's door-yard? Was not the world wide, and was there not room for me outside the charming vale of my nativity?

CHAPTER XVI.

EXCITING NEWS.

My father's common custom of an evening was to adjust his spectacles and read aloud to the family. He was a good reader, and we were all good listeners. We had the usual variety of good literature, with the weekly and daily news; and the times were just exciting enough to command the closest attention to all that was read. Lincoln had been elected to the highest office of the nation; and many had been the speculations as to whether he would safely reach his destination or pass the ordeal of inauguration. In passing to Washington he had seemed to run the guantlet of assassins' knives, while the nation almost held its breath in daily and hourly fear for his security. A few days only had passed since his inaugural when the nation knew that efforts were being made to revictual the forts of the South. This was what the Government had a perfect right to do, and what it was bound in honor to its soldiery to do. But this was accepted as a cause of war by the already organized Confederacy; and orders were issued for the bombardment of Fort Sumter, in Charleston harbor. April 12th the bombardment began; and within thirty-six hours the fort was subdued, and the little garrison of seventy men, under the brave Robert Anderson, marched forth from its battered walls, saluted their honored flag, and shipped for the North.

This, perhaps on the evening of the 14th of April, 1861, was the news read by my father. The head-lines of the announcement ring yet in my ears as pronounced by him in his excited spirit and tones: "OUR FLAG INSULTED! THE WAR ACTUALLY BEGUN! FORT SUMTER BOMBARDED BY THE REBELS!" I jumped to his side, that I might both see and hear all. My mother dropped her work and looked up with a face filled with astonishment. My sisters crouched, as if in fear, at his feet. The headings were read again and again, with the fuller dispatches below. No other news could be read, and the paper was dropped for speculation, indignation, and regrets. I took the paper and read over and over again what I already could have repeated word by word. But words never had such a flaming look to me before. I could not believe them real. Was war, of which I had heard my parents speak so often, war, that horror of the past, actually within the present, my own day, and within our own land? And was this war inaugurated among our own people—American against American? How horrible! And yet amid the actual horror of this scene I felt a relief, such as had not come to me in all my life. Now I could get away from home. I, too, could be a soldier and go forth to battle with the brave. Joy took the place of sadness and despondency in a single moment. I was willing to have my prison door opened, even with the gory key of war. The rebels of Charleston would rescue me from my own home! Did any boy ever before have such crazy thoughts? Was ever another child so foolish as I? I had access to the daily news, which I read with avidity; and I hailed with exceeding ioy the call of the president for 75,000 troops. Captain (afterward colonel) Davis, editor of the *Doylestown Democrat*, was authorized to raise a company for three months. I wished in my heart to enlist, but dared not offer myself, supposing I would not be accepted. How, now, I wished for more years, greater strength, and riper experience. I envied a man, or even one who approached the proportions of manhood. I felt that every one should go, and wondered that any man could be induced to remain at home. The company was soon full, and no more would be received. The day of departure came; the train for their conveyance from Doylestown was ready to start. The solemnity of death as I had never before experienced it seemed to settle on all. Wives were wailing; mothers were weeping; sisters were agonizing beside their loved ones. This was a scene I did not expect, and for which I was not prepared. I had never before witnessed anything that so touched my heart. I could hardly understand why strong men and women should so bow bown with grief on such an occasion. But I knew not then the deep love wherewith heart loved heart, nor the meaning of the tender relationships of life. I could not but weep with those who wept; and yet I silently wished myself among those for whom those tears were being shed. I could have consented that moment to place myself among the soldiery and gaze upon scalding tears in yearning love for myself from the eyes of my own devoted parents. I hoped in my heart that the war would not close until I had age and strength for a soldier. The captain, who was still editor of the *Doylestown Democrat*, weekly forwarded communications from his camp, recounting the services and the experiences of the men. In this I was profoundly interested, and in their perusal I felt myself transported to the front and transformed into a soldier. How happy I thought him, and to me how favored seemed he and his men. To me each man was a hero, one to whom I could have done humblest reverence and yielded richest service.

The city company returned again for the summer, and the excitement of their presence was greater than ever. In their company I felt somewhat reconciled to home. They brought with them the usual variety of literature; and in their genial intelligence they commented on the exciting events of the camp and field, and the home and foreign interests in our war. Their patriotic expressions but served to fire my own military spirit to fever heat. I could not but listen intently to their talk, and yet it but crazed me for a share in the fray. I felt that I was a coward, to remain at home and in security while others fought and bled and died. With avidity I read everything from the front; and the graphic descriptions of the battle scenes were most enjoyable to me. How indignant I felt toward the foes of our men in blue, and how deeply sympathetic for the soldiers of our ranks. Instinctively I would grind my teeth with rage, and reach forth my hand for aid to our faltering fellows. In the flesh I was at home; in spirit, in the camp and upon the battle-field. I tried to drown my restrained feelings in the trashy literature of our company, and by day and night I read the pages of foolish fiction. And yet, in the midst of the most fascinating story, I would dash the paper down and reach forth both hands with a bound for the news from the front. A first perusal never seemed to satisfy me. Again and again would I run the columns over. The old news was ever fresh until that of the coming day was safe in hand.

A lady friend among our company noticing my intense interest in the war-news of the hour, and knowing how ardently I longed for the soldier's life, presented me with a neat soldier-cap. I donned it with pride, and conceived myself fairly crowned at last. I felt myself a soldier, and thought more than ever of the soldier's life. I admired the gift, but most to see my head in a soldier's cap. I felt that it was a surrender of myself in the eyes of my friends and comrades to the cause of my country, and that somehow I was but honoring the men I loved by wearing a cap like theirs.

And now the three months for which our men were enlisted had expired, and it was announced that they would return home. I longed to see them, and yet I hated to have them come. It seemed to me that their coming back was but the signal for the closing of the war. As indignant as I felt toward the rebel, I did not somehow wish him to lay down the arms of his rebellion. The return of the three-months men dried many tears and occasioned much joy. But few had died, and nearly all returned as sound as ever. They were for the time the heroes of the neighborhood; and their description of personal encounters and perilous scenes were animating and exciting to the eager crowd of listeners. I never wearied of their stories, and longed more than ever to see and do what they had seen and done. Nearly all, too, soon longed for further service, and their dissatisfaction and discontent but made me more nervous and uneasy.

CHAPTER XVII.

MORE RECRUITS FOR THE WAR.

In September, Captain (now colonel) Davis began to raise a regiment of men for the war, or for
three years. His camp was established at Doylestown, within four miles of my present home, and
where I had formerly lived. Soon after its establishment I visited camp. This I thought next
thing to enlisting as a soldier, and withal I thought
it a desirable place to be. I would therefor instantly have exchanged the comforts and conven-
iences of my own home—a bed of down for the
barrack of a soldier. What made me more interested in the camp and the life of a soldier from
this moment was the presence of my uncle in
camp. I was rejoiced to see him here. I felt now
that I was at least related to the grand army of
the nation, and that his presence in the camp was
an excuse for and a commendation of my own feelings and wishes. If heretofore I had felt any
compunctions of conscience, they now entirely disappeared. If an uncle could become a soldier and
. 6

leave friends and family, it was certainly right that
I should desire to become one myself.   Thus I felt
that the prospect was brightening for me, and new
joy was enkindled in my breast.   Soon I paid the
camp a second visit, and was delighted to find that
a Mr. Hargrove, whom I knew, was enlisting boys
for the service of drummers.   He wished twenty,
and had already obtained some three or four.   I
went home drumming,—on everything I drummed.
How nice, thought I, to be a drummer-boy.   Surely I was old enough for this service, for some already enlisted were only of my age.   If I could
not carry the gun and draw the saber, I could use
the drum-sticks in calling others to duty and in
inspiring them in their valorous work.

A company of men now came from Reading, and
with them a band of musicians.   Gaining permission, I went again to the camp, which now began
to assume a truly military appearance.   I was delighted with all I saw and with what I heard.   The
music was soul-stirring, and I felt myself called
to duty by the martial strains.   I was electrified,
and felt that I needed but one thing to make me
perfectly happy.   I now formed the resolution that
I would in any event become a soldier of our brave
army.   Life was worth nothing to me, I felt, without the gratification of this wish.   I must go, or I
must pine and die at home.   On reaching home I

expressed my wish and my purpose to my parents. They expressed complete and painful surprise. In this I was disappointed. I knew them to be patriotic, and that they commended others for going. Why, thought I, should they object to my going, and why not rejoice in my purpose? But no; they absolutely refused to entertain even a thought of such a thing. But notwithstanding their refusal, I thought, talked, and dreamed of war and my own service as a soldier. I would often appeal to my father, and beg his consent. He deigned to reason with me, which pained me less than his emphatic refusals. He spoke of the terrors of war, the sufferings of the wounded, and the groans of the dying. He spoke of the crippled soldiers who had, maimed for life, come forth from the war of 1812, and the more recent war with Mexico. But to suffer on the field and return as a cripple was a sort of glory that I felt I could enjoy; while even to die a soldier's death and pass down to an unknown and unmarked grave was an end from which I thought only a coward should shrink. When one's country called in the hour of its peril, what right had a man to the tranquil peace and security of his own fireside, or even to the life he called his own.

My father referred to the opinion of a Rev. Mr. W., as embodying the doubt of the soldier's salva-

tion. Perhaps, if I went to the field, I would sacrifice both my life of earth and that for which I
hoped in heaven. I was simply indignant at the
reverend gentleman for expressing such an opinion,
and was in no wise convinced by his logic. I was
willing to accept every chance and every risk of
a soldier, and felt too little regard for the consequences following his life, either here or hereafter.
As a final argument, my father said—and why, I
do not know, and could not then understand,—that
I might lose my sight; that if I went to the field I
might return from the service *blind*. This suggestion made an impression on me as none of the
other arguments had. I had a horror of the very
thing suggested; and perhaps knowing this, and
remembering my sympathy for the blind Professor
Dyer, he thought to mention the thing.

I, however, went again to camp, and tried to enlist. They would not accept me without the written consent of my parents. I knew too well that
for their consent I could not hope. I had now
gone as far as I could, and was somewhat quieted
in my own feelings. If the Government *would*
not have me, of course I was justified in remaining
at home. Still I was not satisfied, and constantly
hoped on as before. If I had consented to stifle
my feelings, I could not long have repressed them.
Recruiting meetings were being held often in the

Baptist church of our village; and the pastor, Mr. Wheat, was an earnest advocate of enlistments. What he could approve I felt myself justified in. The patriotic flame within me was fanned into a furious life.

The regiment was now full, and a flag presentation transpired. How grand the old banner seemed as soldier hands unfurled it, and as soldier hearts and lips honored it with the rousing " three times three." To defend the flag, and if need be to die under its folds, were professions that but endeared the men and added to my earnest regard for their cause. Their parade, with music floating upon the breeze, with perfect step to the time of their tune, and with their dear banner unfurled for the kiss of heaven, endeared them to my heart, and but increased my longing desire to be one with them. What an inspiring sight was that of their march and their drill! Who could behold it and not wish to share in the service, so honorable in the eyes of the world and so gloried over by the patriotic of the the nation ?

After the parade the distribution of Testaments was gone through with, and each soldier became possessed of the precious word. How fitting, I thought, for men who are to battle for their country to possess, also, the sword of the Spirit. I was glad to see this distribution, for the good it did those who gave them and for the good I thought it must do those who received them. The Bible never seemed more precious to me than then, and never before did I so understand its value. It also seemed to me as if it were never in better hands, in many ways, than when borne in the palms of those men in blue. The gun and the Bible, I thought, were fitting companions in this case, when the soldiery sought not the subjugation of a foe, but the salvation of the land and the perpetuation of the republic. If such a soldier had not a right to that *treasure*, and if for the soldier its lessons were not, then had I misunderstood its import and overvalued its merit. The American soldier's Bible, I felt then, was the word of God. Therein has he justification, and therefrom may he have comfort.

And now the time of leave-taking had come. A thousand men were to go forth from the camp at home to the field, among strangers. I was especially interested in this departure. Many of my comrades were in the ranks,—boys a little my senior, beside whom I had sat in day and Sunday school, and with whom I had shared the richer sports of my youthful days I was to bid them good-bye, and stay behind. I rejoiced that they were going; I honored, I loved, and yet I envied them. With my parents, I rode to Doylestown; and soon the long train was drawn up, and the men, with mirth and glee commingled with tears and even groans, had boarded the cars for their departure. Sad was the sight; and it grieved me much that hearts should ache and tears should flow. My parents wept in silence for the grief of others, and perhaps in thought of coming woe for themselves. I could not consent that these men should go and leave me. My first determination was to board the train in the moment of starting; but I knew that if I did I should be put off, and thus disgraced. But when they were finally gone, when no longer we could hear the stifled good-bye, nor see in the distance the waving handkerchief, then my heart was aflame with anger. I was even boiling with rage; and this madness was against my parents. I felt that they had kept me back, and were wholly and only responsible for my disappointment. In this act, how foolish was I and how full of devotion were they. They knew wherein was my peace, and that I sought as a child the path of woe and misery. Had I been honest, I would have confessed their love in restraining my rashness. I would not join them in the homeward ride, but chose, in my vengeful and sullen spirit, to walk the distance alone. Arriving late at home, I went to bed in a pout, caring not to extend either the good-night kiss or word

CHAPTER XVIII.

SYMPATHY AND CARE FOR THE SOLDIER.

And now the regiment was gone, and therewith, for the present, almost the *last* hope of my heart. The boarders, too, who had measurably brought an outside world into our home, had also gone. Home had less charms than ever, and the world seemed to have turned its back forever on one of its humble children. I imagined I had no friends, and that all were false to me. But cold winter was coming on, and the men who had left their homes of comfort and plenty for the gloomy fields of southern strife began to be in want; and the pleading voice for aid came up to the deserted homes and their weeping, wailing inmates. They missed the delicate bounties of their not-forgotten tables; and their feet especially were suffering from the cold.

Knitting became an almost universal employment; and it seemed as though even the men would again learn an art now lost to them. Knitting parties were the order, while every housewife found time to fashion the wool of the sheep into stockings for the brave boys in blue. Boxes were hastily prepared and filled with supplies for the men, wherein many were remembered much, but all were remembered some. Even the stranger was not forgotten, though he had no wife, no sister, no mother to whom to address his appeal. How happy the people felt in the act of offering, and how consecrated everything sent seemed to be. Never had priest more effectually blessed sacred things than did our women at home bless each little article marked and named for the absent soldier. Such wonderful outgushings of sympathy, and such devout and tender expressions of love, I had never before witnessed. It seemed to me that all love now was for the absent ones, and that to be loved one must pass on to the perils of the front. The men at home appeared ashamed; and while the women wept for the absent, they appeared manifestly indifferent toward the able-bodied who remained at home. If news came that one was sick in camp, even if at home no one regarded him, from every heart came expressions of sympathy, and every one appeared ready to be transformed into his guardian angel. If a soldier died, all became mourners, and the world seemed to turn out for the burial of his body, if it could be brought home. Never were saints so eulo-

gized, even from the sacred desk, as was the soldier
who happened to die in camp or on the field; and
one was almost adjudged a criminal who dared to
say, or even think, that the soldier, whatever his
character, was unsaved. In the *blue*, under the
banner, appeared to guaranty him a passport
through the gates of life.

This devotion only served to increase my en-
thusiastic admiration for the soldier's life, and to
fix my purpose to enter the war at the earliest moment. I envied the soldiers beyond all other men,
and thought them the happiest of mortals. My
father now began to admonish me against further
thought of the service, and to congratulate me that
I was not numbered with the suffering men. But
his talk made no impression on me. I felt that
there was a glory in their want and suffering that
made it intensely enjoyable and desirable; and
while I could pity, I envied them none the less.
To congratulate myself was but to call up the spirit
of a coward in my heart, and to willingly resign
the very glory for which I thirsted. My mother
expressed much happiness over my home presence,
and blessed God with her daily life that her dear
boy was not on the tented field. Her happiness
from this source was but the fire for further anger
with me. It was joy, as I thought, at my expense,
and delight at my disappointment. How hard

was my judgment, I had occasion at no distant day
to fully understand.   I recalled, with bitter weeping, my own hardness of heart, but not, however,
until the shadow had quite gone over the broken
heart of my mother.

CHAPTER XIX.

A SOLDIER AT LAST.

For one more winter I was in school; and oh, that I could have known and realized that it was my last! Could I have been told as much I would have rejoiced with wildest joy. No prophecy would have pleased me better. School was but a prison for me, and its walls but those of a dungeon. I believe I would have exchanged them even for those of cold and dismal Libby, or the death-dealing field of Andersonville. In them I saw glory, and that upon them the eyes of a nation rested in sympathy. How weak the judgment and how foolish the ambition that begrudged the dying, starving soldier-prisoner his glory; that for it would exchange the love of home, the attention of friends, and the advantages of school! Improve I would not, and advance I did not. To learn my lessons and improve my mind was too much like condescension to my teachers, and gratification for my parents. I only longed for the close of the day and for the end of the term. I was angry at every one, and was even mad at my self for betraying a weakness that admitted of defeat. If I could not battle on the field, I would fight at home; if I could not face the *rebel*, I would face, in foolish fury, my mates. I actually took comfort in wicked brawls and daily fights. To whip or be whipped was all the same, and seemed to satify for the moment my foolish ambition for glory. If friends would not release me because of their love, I would even loosen those love-bands, and change the spirit that inspired them into one of indifference and hate. It was love, I knew, that held me, and because of this I even hated to be loved.

Captain Harvey, in the midwinter, opened a recruiting office at Doylestown, and frequently the sound of drum and fife was heard in my home. I was charmed with the music and re-inspired with its strains. I learned that a mate of mine, a drummer-boy, was to be sent home, and the thought occurred to me that possibly I might be accepted in his place. I would go to Doylestown and offer myself at least. If rejected, I would feel a satisfaction in the fact and thought of the offer and the effort. From school I went over to Doylestown, arriving about dark, tired and hungry. Entering the office, there stood the captain, a tall, gray-haired, soldierly-looking man, writing at his desk,

and alone. My heart was in my throat at sight of
him, for it seemed to me that in him centered all
the happiness for which I hoped. I mustered
courage, however, at once, and said, "Captain, do
you want a drummer-boy, in place of Bobby
Bryon? Scanning me from head to foot, and
almost piercing me with his eyes, he said, "What,
sir, can you do?" Hanging my head and scraping
my feet, I answered, "I think I could learn to
drum, sir." "Did you ever drum any?" he asked
again. I bethought myself of a toy-drum that I
had had a few years before, and I instantly answered, "I have drummed a little, sir." "But you
are too small, my boy." "I think that I can stand
it if I am, if the rest can." "Well, I will see."
And he began writing again. I began to hope
somewhat; but withal, I was tormented with
doubts as yet unsettled. That he would take me
I did not know. Respectfully I sat in silence, not
wishing by any impertinence to diminish my
chances for acceptance. Men began to enter the
office and address different inquiries to the captain
regarding the service, and some enrolled their
names for soldiers. But the evening was passing; and I was hungry, and a long distance from
home. I feared the captain had entirely forgotten
me, and so at last, half despairing, I summoned
courage to address him again. "Captain." said I,

"Can you tell me now if I will answer for a drummer-boy?" His answer chilled my heart. "I can not think of taking you without the written consent of both your parents. However, consult them, and see me again in a day or two." Without any reason, I dared hope they would consent, and I said, "If they are willing, can I go?" He would only answer, "I will see." I entered upon my return walk with a heavy heart somewhat lightened, yet fearful of disappointment at last. My folks were in bed, for the hour of midnight was near. I passed a restless night, and slept only to dream of army life and myself as a soldier therein. I arose with the early dawn, determining to make the best use of the day. I petitioned my father, and begged him for his consent, but with no shadow of success. I spent many hours in drumming, with hands and sticks, on everthing.

A few days had elapsed, and no concession had been made by my parents. I thought to write a permit and sign it myself, but could not get the courage happily to do this.

One evening, at the end of a week, I came home and found father reading, but not in a specially happy mood. I pleaded with him again, until at last his patience seemed exhausted, and to my joyful surprise he took up a piece of note-paper and hastily wrote a permit and signed it. He handed it to me and said, "Now, get your mother to sign it if you can." He felt that now he had rid himself, of further trouble, and had transferred me to another court, whereat I could gain no point or have any hope. He had judged well of my mother. He knew she would not let me go. I felt that I was hopelessly approaching the new tribunal, and yet I was rejoiced that I had the consent of one. I would make the best use of this. I pleaded with my mother, cried, and finally threatened to run away from home. She looked at me in silence through her scalding tears and answered, unmistakably and emphatically, "*no!*" I could not long face her tears, and was glad to go out from her presence, even without her consent.

My mother's refusal gratified my father, and he appeared to feel that now the trouble was at an end. I was rebuked, but did not feel myself defeated. I thought, planned, and plotted cautiously. I knew there was no further use in pleading with my mother, and that I could never obtain her consent. I would see how far my father's single permission would carry me. A week passed, and one evening I went to the station; and being without money I took my seat, as the cars were starting, on the rear platform of the last car, and passed on to Doylestown unobserved.

The captain and a drummer-boy named Kelley were at the depot, and I walked with them to the office. Entering, I at once pulled out my father's permit and said, "Here, captain, I have it." He read it and said to my relief, "That will do, sir; I will swear you in after supper." After his return, Kelley and I were sworn in and sent to the hotel to remain until we could be prepared and sent on to the front. My heart was filled with remorse, commingled with a joyful satisfaction. I was a soldier now, and belonged to the service of my country. But I knew too well that I had acted dishonorably, and that the captain's course was without proper warrant, and even beyond his own promise. Before retiring I had the captain's permission to go home in the morning and spend the Sabbath with my folks. I slept but little, and before the light was at the train for my home. I arrived home before my mother was up, but father was building the fire. I touched his shoulder and said, in almost a whisper, "I have enlisted." "Oh, wicked boy," said he, "you will break your father's heart." There was anguish in his look, and a burning reproof, like fire, on his words, for me. When my mother came down, she was almost crushed with the news, and shed bitterest tears, in which I could not but join with her. I feared they would protest, and at once take steps to undo what I had done; but of this they said nothing.

7

The Sabbath-day was devoted to a visit to my mother's father. I can not say that I enjoyed the stay, as so much of the time was given to the thought of my action and final leaving home. My mother was so full of sorrow that I could not be happy. Still, for her sake, I could not have retraced my steps or recalled my oath to the government. The morning came at last, and I bid the loved ones, now doubly loved, what proved to be a final good-bye. All malice now had departed from my heart. I was loving the home circle with the tender love I had formerly indulged for them. I was not sorry when the hour of departure had come, as the sorrow of the visit was unmanning me, and I felt that I could restrain my feelings but little longer.

I returned to the hotel at Doylestown, where bar-room talk somewhat mitigated my grief. A few days after my return, as I went into the dining hall, there sat my mother in the corner of the room, silently weeping. She looked care-worn, and yet in her sadness doubly beautiful and lovely. My heart was sick at her sight, and I was almost glad to hear her say that she could stay but a moment. I was, she said, to return home on the morrow, and she must hurry back, that she might have my things in readiness. In her love she had prepared many little things for me to take, and all would be ready at my coming. Since protesting had not been effectual, affection had been busy in preparing for my comfort. Little I knew the fervency of that mother's love, the depth of her pure affection. Her's was a *mother's* love, and this explained it all.

Soon after she left us marching orders came, and instead of going home for a day I could simply pass by my father's home on my way to the front. At first I was pained by my disappointment, and then this feeling gave way to relief. I dreaded the thought of returning home for the final good-bye. I did not longer feel guilty, but I felt that I could stand no more tears, and that in the final farewell my mother's heart would break. I did not have opportunity to even get word to my parents, that they might meet me on the passing train at the station.

CHAPTER XX.

OFF TO THE FRONT.

The day of departure had come. Some thirty of us were to go forward to the 104th regiment as recruits. Among these was a soldier who deeply regretted having enlisted. To drown his grief he used the cup. He tried to get away, and begged to be released. This, however, could not be; and that he might be safe when the train arrived he was firmly tied. In this condition he was taken aboard the cars. When passing the old home I hoped I should see all the loved ones. I was almost dying for one look more at mother, father, sisters, and brother. But as the train dashed by I saw only a sister, to whom I threw my bundle of old clothes and a kiss of affection for her and all. And now, on the swift wings of steam I was leaving home, and perhaps forever. My father's words rung in my ears,—perhaps I would be crippled, lose my sight, or possibly my life, and therewith my soul. My mother's sad look haunted me, and the vision, with all my love for her, made me sick at heart. But my wish was answered; I was accepted as a soldier in the service of my country. I would know now what the world was, and whether the dreams of fancy, as inspired by the pages of the poisonous *New York Ledger*, were indeed real. Home, in these moments, began to appear the sacred place that it really was; and while I then wished no return to it, yet I deeply mourned that I had not loved and appreciated it better; that in striving to get from home I had really sought to poison the atmosphere of home.

In the midst of these reveries, Philadelphia was reached, where we had a stay of a few hours only. Little thought I then what experiences I was to have within its borders. The future was graciously shadowed by a merciful Providence. While I was content with my lot, and longed to be again on the wing, my drummer-mate, Kelley, was not so happy. He had begun to regret the practical expression of his patriotism by enlistment. He longed to be free again. Already he had seen enough of soldier life. But we were all closely guarded in our waiting-room, and escape was difficult. In the winking of an eye, however, Kelley was through the window and on the run, a free young man, as he supposed. But he had little chance to answer his wish. His speed and ap-

pearance both aroused suspicion, and he was soon
caught and returned by an officer. He was weeping bitterly when brought in, and as a punishment
was locked up and closely guarded.

Soon onward again we sped, and in good time
reached Baltimore City. At last I felt that I was
indeed on bloody ground. I remembered vividly
the account of the Baltimore riot of the previous
19th of April; and I instinctively felt that I could
see traces of blood for the looking. There was little time for observation, however, or for speculation, the only thing of real interest occurring to us
in the city being the second attempted escape of
my comrade, Kelley. This time he attempted to
jump from the train as it was moving out, but was
caught in the act by one of our soldiers and returned again to our car. From this time he was
allowed little liberty, being closely watched until
our arrival in camp. I pitied him from my heart,
and half wished he might succeed in his endeavor.
I felt that one should be free in this matter of
military service; and he being young, I felt anger-
ed almost that he should be pursued.

A brief ride, and we were in Washington, a city
that seemed sacred to me from its name and its re-
lation to the nation. It appeared to me now that I
was resting against the throbbing heart of my country. The sight of the grand old capitol of the na-

tion, under whose dome the politically great of the
country and the world had so often gathered,
thrilled me with a new interest. Could American
citizens, I could reason, but stand to-day under the
shadow of their nation's capitol, how the fires of
patriotism would burn within them, and how quickly would the thousands needed for the crushing of
the rebellion come to the front for the solemn af-
fray. I felt that it was well to march our men to
the field by the grand and beautiful structure, if
not through its majestic portals. But we could
take no time for observation, except such as we
could glean on the wing. We were pushed on to
Kaloroma Heights, a few miles from Georgetown,
where we found our regiment.

CHAPTER XXI.

CAMP-LIFE.

I was now in camp, and began to realize the solemn truth that I was a soldier at last. As in my weariness I lay down in my tent that night, I had strange feelings indeed. I thought of home now as the sweetest, dearest, and most sacred spot of earth; but perhaps I had forever passed its threshold. Mother, father, sisters, and brother passed in rapid and constantly-recurring vision; and I saw plainly how in ten thousand ways they had shown their love for me. But oh, how ill had I requited them. These thoughts I was glad to banish at last through the help of sleep—"tired nature's sweet restorer." With the first light of the morn I began to make a closer inspection of my surroundings. The outward appearance of the men greatly disappointed me. I had seen them only in the camp of instruction, and when clothing and accouterments were all new. But the dust and dirt of camp, together with the careless indifference of the men since beyond the watchful eyes of home friends, had greatly changed the appearance of all. The camp was pleasant, and the surrounding country delightful. With all this, however, I was soon full of fear and homesickness. There was much sickness, including small-pox, in the camp. I had of this greatly more fear than I had of the rebels, and I felt equally sure that I should fare no better at its hands should I be taken down. I found, too, that I had undertaken more than I thought—to learn the art of drumming in the soldier's camp and for the service of the field. For the first month I made but poor proficiency, and felt very much discouraged over my slow progress. Still, I was ambitious, and reasonably persevering, and was sure that in time I would master my art.

Soon after New-Years we removed our regiment to the barracks in Camp Carver, about three miles from Washington, and a like distance from the Soldiers' Home. Our camp accommodated four regiments and a company of artillery. The barracks, consisting of some twelve houses to a regiment, formed the outer lines of a square, inclosing perhaps ten acres of level ground, with the old flag waving from a central staff. On the east side of this square was the 104th Pennsylvania, on the south the 52d Pennsylvania, on the west the 56th New York, and on the north the 11th Maine.

The Columbia Hospital was situated near our

camp, and from it to the cemetery the road passed directly in front of our regiment. Daily funerals, accompanied by the solemn, muffled drum, and the sad ringing of the hospital bell, attracted for a time my most serious and painful attention. With these solemn processions sometimes five or six bodies were carried to burial at one time, and not unfrequently several processions passed us in a single day. Letters from home came often, and breathed for me the tenderest possible spirit. At first their arrival awakened unhappy emotions, and sometimes I wished myself at home again. But I was being fast weaned from home, and even from the thoughts and habits of a goodly life. There were a few faithful ones in camp, and they, with the chaplain, kept up the weekly service and prayer-meeting, but I rarely attended them. If duty called me toward the chaplain's tent or the place of prayer, I hurriedly passed them by.

With my separation from home friends, and the sad scenes of death and burial all around me, with the early prospect of perhaps fatal conflict with the enemy, all of these considerations should certainly have awakened and continued serious emotions. Very soon, however, I could say, "None of these things move me." I was fast becoming an unprincipled and hardened boy. I was in that school least of all suited to myself, and where thousands, for time and eternity, were hopelessly ruined. Card-playing, the soldier's curse, as well as the fatal curse of society at home, and penny-poker, became my daily amusement. At first there were scruples of conscience, remembering the aversion of my parents to this habit, and the convictions of my own heart. Soon, however, these were stifled, and I felt little trouble in doing as others did. A few faithful men admonished me, and for a day or two I would regard their counsels and heed their warnings, but soon the jeerings of comrades would rally me again to their sports. At the card-table I soon learned its usual language, and became at last a profane swearer. This was wholly against my purpose, but when once angry I found that I could go any distance.

My drummer-mate, Cochran, was a Catholic boy, raised in New York. I did not like him any too well; but our service threw us together, and as mates we would often share the social game of cards, even to the extent of gambling. One day we became enraged, and a fight was the conclud-ing episode of the game. We were arrested and taken to the captain's head-quarters for punish-ment. We were handcuffed hand to hand and face to face. This was too much for foes, and a nearness of communion that neither of us admired.

For an hour or so we kicked at and spit upon each other, until at last we were both exhausted and ashamed. Anger ceased, and friendship became cordial and permanent from that hour. Toward night, after being thus handcuffed for nearly an entire day, we were released on the promise that we would play penny-poker no more. The promise, though made in good faith, was soon broken, and the exciting game renewed with new interest and enthusiasm for a time. Meantime letters were arriving every week from home; and though I ever rejoiced in their coming, yet it seemed as though they had eyes to see and lips to declare my conduct to mourning loved ones at home. Hardened, as I had already become, I was far from willing that my folks should know the condition of my heart and recklessness of my conduct.

Several times while in this camp boxes from the loved ones at home arrived, laden with rich and enjoyable tokens of comfort. Once I was deeply affected in being thus remembered by my Sabbath-school mates. While these delicacies comforted, they also condemned me, as I felt myself wholly unworthy of the bestowments. I had come to enjoy camp-life. My improvement on the drum had made of that labor a pleasure, while boxing, card-playing, pitching pennies, smoking, etc., had become fixed and foolish habits with me. I ever

thought that I would leave them all in the camp,
and that I should never wish to indulge them when
again at home. But habits once formed, I was to
learn, were not so easily broken, and though adopt-
ed for a day, might continue even for a life-time.
The measles during the spring were very common
and fatal in our camp. The Maine regiment lost
nearly if not quite one half of their men. In
our regiment they also prevailed widely and fatal-
ly. Our two marker-boys were down with them,
and were taken to the hospital. They seemed to
do well, and soon were both out again and in camp.
They came to camp together; and both of them, the
first night, took cold and the following day relapsed
and died. This was a shocking and chilling spectacle. It reminded me of my recklessness and
my complete lack of preparation. I was the more
uneasy as I had not had the measles myself. Soon
I, too, was down, and at once too sick to be removed to the hospital. I began to think that perhaps my time had come, and that possibly I had
seen home and family friends for the last time.
Bitter remorse took hold upon me, and I vowed a
better life for the future should I recover. And
God in good time raised me up again.

CHAPTER XXII.

MARCHING TO THE BATTLE-FIELD.

I was no sooner about the camp than marching orders were received. We crossed Long Bridge about dusk, and continued our march most of the night. Much of the way I had to be led, from weakness and partial loss of sight. We went into camp toward morning, near Alexandria, Virginia, and remained two days and nights without our tents, exposed to rain and snow. Our condition was fearfully bad, and the heartiest suffered much from the exposure. From my condition it was exceedingly hard on me, and led, doubtless, to consequences which were fully ripened only in my ultimate blindness.

We were now ordered into Alexandria, the scene of the recent death of the lamented young Ellsworth. This young man, at the time of his death, was engaged to be married to Miss Spafford, of Rockford, Illinois, a decendent of General Warren, who was killed at Bunker Hill. Had this marriage transpired before he entered the service, as was intended, then the first officer that fell in the Revolution and the first that fell in the Rebellion would have had relationship through marriage. The old stairway whereon Ellsworth was killed, and which was stained with his precious blood, had been literally chipped to pieces and carried away as bits of sacred relics. New stairs now replaced the old. We were directed to board the Constitution, a Pacific mail-steamer, where four regiments lay for the night. The river was rough, the wind was wild, and the storm poured with unceasing fury. Our regiment was above, on the hurricane deck, and we were protected for a time by an awning; but before morning this yielded under its vast weight of water, and as a result we were completely drenched. Several times, too, the vessel nearly capsized from the weight of the men; and withal the night was a fearful lapse of time. It was evident that the vessel was too heavily loaded, and with the dawn two of our regiments were marched ashore. After a few hours we boarded another steamer, the State of Maine, for Fortress Monroe. There was little of interest in the downward passage, except that it gave me my first experience at sea-going and steamer-sailing. The scenery was grand, and had I felt well I could have enjoyed it much. Our passage near to the resting-place of Washington, at Mt. Vernon, awakened sacred memories, and stirred within us the patriotic fires. The thought that his grave was in dust claimed by the so-called Confederacy was calculated to inspire a sentiment of devotion to the old flag under which and for which he fought, and to awaken within all new ardor in our cause. Many a soldier has written on his heart fresh vows, and consecrated himself anew on his country's altar, as he has passed near the shadows of Mt. Vernon..

I was much exhausted on my arrival at the fortress, as was my drummer-mate. We were both urged to go to the hospital; but he had to go alone, I refusing to go. We went into camp at Newport News, where we arrived about sundown. I was too weak to carry my knapsack, which one of the captains kindly volunteered to carry for me. The regiment almost immediately moved toward Yorktown; but for nearly a week I remained at the News, unfit for duty, and too weak to go forward. After entering camp near Yorktown I suffered extremely from my eyes, and was, of course, of little or no account to the regiment. It began to be painfully evident to me that as a soldier I could render but little service and be of little value. This I deeply regretted, as the flame of patriotism was all aglow within me. Our regiment was engaged in daily reconnoitering expeditions, and suf-

fered from an occasional casualty. Occasionally
shells from the enemies' guns would pass over and
near our camp. This awakened a sentiment of
fear within me for about the first time. While
lying here letters from home conveyed the sad
news of my father's sickness. He had broken an
arm. I began to suffer from remorse. If I had
stayed at home I could give both help and comfort
now; but as I was I could be of benefit to no one,
and knew full well that I occasioned much sorrow
and anxiety to the loved ones at home.

Yorktown was finally evacuated by the rebels,
and our forces advanced in pursuit. I was left behind with the baggage guard. After the severely-
earned victory of Williamsburg our regiment went
into camp at White House, on the Pamunky.
There we went by steamer to join them; but on our
arrival we found they had left in pursuit of the enemy. After a wearying search of two days we finally
found them near Savage Station, across the Chickahominy. Being now somewhat recovered, I reported for duty. We were constantly engaged in
reconnoitering, and were in daily expectation of
engaging the enemy. Our regiment met the enemy from this point in a slight skirmish, which
proved their first experience under fire. Several
were wounded, and one man was killed. The account was exceedingly exciting to me, and I felt

8

vengeful blood coursing through my veins. The
enemy was reported near, and anxious for battle
on their chosen ground. We now removed to Fair
Oaks, where we were in hourly expectation of a
battle. A rebel sharp-shooter was here brought into
camp severely wounded. His presence excited
savage indignation among the men. Preparations
were now being hurriedly made for a final engagement. Baggage was sent to the rear, across the
Chickahominy. The engagement was begun by
the enemy, and our regiment, from the first, was
in the thickest of the fight. The shells came fearfully close to us, and I was in momentary expectation of being killed. The noise of the artillery
and musketry was absolutely deafening, while our
forces for a time were driven back and through
our camp, which was occupied by the enemy. All
was confusion, as may well be imagined; and I began to desire some place of safety. My work was
not exciting enough to inspire courage. Wounded
men were being carried hurriedly to the rear,
mangled, groaning, and dying. The spectacle was
horrifying. I did not join our regiment again until sundown. Great as was their danger, I felt
somewhat secure in their company. But how
changed their appearance! From six hundred
strong in the morning, now only about a hundred
and twenty-five answered roll-call. Darkness had

brought the battle to a close. Our men were ordered into the rifle-pits, and directed to hold them
until re-enforcements could arrive. Re-enforcements did come to their relief during the night,
but not until late. I spent much of the night in
assisting the wounded men. In the morning the
enemy was driven back and our camp recovered.

My visit to the camp and battle-field was blood-
curdling indeed. The wounded had nearly all
been removed, and mostly by the enemy, but the
dead remained for us to bury. The sight was horrible, and the stench already sickening. Men and
horses were piled everywhere in confusion, and
mangled in the most shocking manner. Some
were pierced only by the bullet, and looked peaceful and human in death, while others were torn
almost to atoms. In many parts of the field the
blue and the gray were mingled together, sleeping
side by side in death like friends, though bitterest
foes in life. On one spot, about fifteen feet square,
I counted twenty dead men; and these masses of
dead were common. They had gone down under
the fire of grape; and winnows had been made in
their ranks. In many instances a group of men
would be lying dead under the shade and protection of a tree, whither as wounded men they had
crowded, and where at last, in agony and without
attention, they had died. For those whom we

could recognize we dug single graves, and marked
their places of slumber.   For the unrecognized we
dug trenches, and buried them three and four deep.
Often the dead of both sides were commingled in
the same grave, thus to sleep until the resurrection
awakening.

We now removed to Dispatch Station; but of
our camp fixtures nothing was worth the taking.
If anything of value had escaped, the enemy had
appropriated it.   Again the battle raged, and once
more our forces were pushed across the Chickahominy.   A night was spent in the rifle-pits.   The
enemy's shells were falling about us.   Evidently
our army was preparing to recross and retreat.
All night baggage trains were passing to the rear,
and the cannonading was changing its location and
toward our lines.   Morning came at last.   I was
suffering intensely from my eyes.   I eat my breakfast on a grave-tablet; and in my hunger I enjoyed it none the less.   Our ordnance-master, J. W.
McCoy, an early school-mate, approached and gave
me sympathy.   Said he, "This is no place for a
sick boy;" and he urged me to the rear, assuring
me that there would be warm work before the day
was closed.   He also loaned me his glass, through
which I could see the enemy across the river, strongly intrenched.   He wrote me a pass, and gave directions for my route to the rear.   He then kindly

volunteered the use of his horse for my journey. This favor filled me with gratitude. It was but one of a hundred favors, however, recorded in my heart as from him. By this act, I feel sure he saved my life. His memory is most sacred to me. I had a brisk ride of several hours, along gurgling brooks, through waving groves, and by golden grain-fields, amid the warbling of happy birds. I saw no one but a few negroes on the route. They were friendly, but shy. A ride of ten miles brought me to the main body of our troops in retreat. I delivered my horse, as directed, to the wagon-master, and continued with the army in their retreat until night, emcamping at White Oak Swamps. I remained in camp next day amid the roar of battle, when with a column of men I began my rearward march. I was soon exhausted, and must have lain down by the way had not an ammunition-wagon driver kindly offered me a ride. He bid me lie low in his wagon, that I might not be observed. This was not a comfortable position, nor one of special security, but I was most grateful for it. I reached Malvern Hill in the night, and here remained until near the close of the long-continued battle, when I went to Harrison's Landing, on the James, and with others encamped on the grounds of a planter's home. The mansion, overseer's home, and the cabins of the negroes were filled with the wounded and sick, and the grounds were covered with tents for their further accommodation. Our encampment reached to the water's edge; and all was under the protection of the gun-boats.

CHAPTER XXIII.

NORTHWARD AND HOMEWARD.

Soon after my arrival our regimental surgeon called me to his head-quarters and told me that from my prostrated condition and the bad state of my eyes he had concluded to send me north, to stay until I was somewhat restored. This was welcome news indeed; and I asked him if I could be sent home to my father's, but was disappointed in his saying that I must go to some hospital, where I could receive treatment for my eyes. In a few hours he had accompanied me to a boat, the City of New York, loaded with sick and wounded soldiers. I met with cordial expressions of sympathy and ready attention from the officers, surgeons, and nurses. Dr. Hartshorn, a surgeon from Philadelphia, was among the passengers, and showed me very special attention. He inquired my name and place of residence, kindly examined my eyes, and procured me many needed comforts on the voyage. At sunset we started down the river. I felt almost guilty in leaving the brave men who were struggling with the foe under such discouraging circumstances; yet I could no longer be of service, and would only receive attention that others stood sadly in need of. I was delighted with the idea of going toward home, and thought that possibly I might soon see loved faces again.

All went well for a few miles, when just as the darkness was closing around us a light, as of lightning, flashed shoreward, and the same instant a shot whistled over our deck. A rebel battery had assailed us. Several shots passed over us, and two passed through the vessel. All was excitement, and a hasty retreat was beaten. Fortunately no one was hurt, and the danger was soon over. A friendly gun-boat was close behind us, which soon cleared the shore of the malicious intruder, and we were enabled to proceed down the river without further molestation. For a day or two we tarried at Fortress Monroe, receiving coal and otherwise preparing for our voyage. During the journey little of interest transpired beyond the deaths of perhaps a dozen of our sick and wounded. We committed none of them to watery graves, as I supposed would be the case, but all were preserved for burial on land. I was intensely anxious to know our destination, but I could learn from no one. At last however, we were steaming up a river which, to my joy, I learned to be the Delaware. We were making for Philadelphia, and soon were at anchor before the wharf. Here an immense crowd of anxious friends were gathered, looking for or seeking to learn of their loved ones. All were soon ashore but myself and another boy. The meeting of friends occasioned wild bursts of joy from many, while others stood in silence and sorrow, weeping that their loved ones had not come and might never return.

While the wounded were being removed I recognized among the crowd pressing on the boat in search of friends a Mr. Green, who had formerly spent a season with us as a summer boarder. He knew me at once, and desired to take me to his home and care for me there. But the doctor had forbidden my leaving the boat; and when Mr. G. pressed his request, he denied, as he insisted, in my own interest. With the other boy, I was sent to the Episcopal Hospital, in the city, where I was cordially received and kindly cared for. Here my medical attendance was of the best order, and my spiritual surroundings were all that could be wished. Rev. Mr. Paddock was chaplain of the institution, and gave me careful, spiritual attention.

After a few days' rest I obtained permission to return home. I was now so near home that I could not longer content myself. I was overjoyed at the prospect, but kept all from my parents, even the fact of my arrival in Philadelphia. Several weeks, indeed, had elapsed since I had written to them; and in the confusion of retreat and travel, together with my actual, personal suffering, I had neglected the small opportunities that seemed to offer. Taking the train, I was soon nearing home once more. I determined to avoid observation, and make my arrival a complete surprise. I soon left the car, and being acquainted with the engineer, I went aboard the engine. I had, however, been seen and recognized by an old gentleman; and, as if to give the earliest possible joy, he hurried to apprise my family of my coming. I did not leave the engine until the passengers had all alighted, and then I started directly for home. How I felt, God only knows. There was the old school-house, where I had taken, as a student, my first lessons. Near by was the church where we had often worshiped; and yonder was my own dear home, wherein were father, mother, sisters, and brother, unconscious, as I supposed, of my presence. If living, I knew their hearts were full of love for me. The life that had been so recklessly spent had been preserved, and I was now almost within the shadow of the old home. I was happy amid my penitence, and mourned and rejoiced together. When within a square or so of the house I saw my fa-

ther emerge from the door and start toward me
on the run. His now whitened locks were streaming in the wind, while in sobbing tones he was
crying, "My boy, my boy." He took me into his
arms and pressed me to his bosom. Now, hand in
hand, we walked in the silence of weeping toward
the house. Mother, sisters, and Willie met me before the door, all crying for joy, and greeted me
with the same affection my father had shown.
We walked into the house and sat down in silence,
a silence disturbed only by the broken sobs of all. I
thought myself a prodigal indeed. The prodigal had
been greeted no more cordially than was I. Like
him, I had wandered far from the fold, only to return and find myself unforgotten, still loved with
immeasurable affection, and the recipient of the
best that each and all could give. The recklessness of my own course was now lamented and repented of with scalding tears and penitent prayers;
and I thought, never again will I do as in my
wickedness I have heretofore done.

The next day was Sabbath, and it was determined that we should all go to church and hear Dr. Andrews, with a thank-offering in our hearts to God.
As we passed into the house of God I obtained a
view of the grave of my brother Ross; and while I
missed the dear, dear boy, I thought him happy
that he had not lived to see and know the world

as I had seen and known it. Surely, death in the sweet days of innocence leaves a record unmarred for eternity's retrospections; and the soul must lift itself in joyful praise to God while indulging the blissful thought, "*I have never sinned.*" Never could I say this; but I dared hoped that yet, by his side, I might say, "I have repented all my sins, and they are forgiven me by the precious Lamb whose blood has atoned for them." How precious to me the spot where he rested; how sacred the dust to which his infant body had returned. How solemn, too, seemed the house of God, and how welcome the face and voice of the minister at the altar. I felt, indeed, that I was in a sacred place; and in my heart I thanked God for one more such Sabbath-day, and its worship by the side of my father's family.

My leave of absence covered but ten days; and these fleeting days were well and happily improved. Friends came from all sections and directions, variously inquiring after their own loved ones, and wishing the rehearsal of my own experience. My own friends were visited, not forgetting the home of my grandfather Martin, where my last Sabbath at home had been spent. The days glided but too swiftly, and were speedily gone, necessitating my return to the hospital.

CHAPTER XXIV.

HOSPITAL LIFE AND LEAVE OF THE ARMY.

Their new building was now completed, and in this I took up my home. Soon some sixty exchanged prisoners from Libby arrived, mostly wounded, many of whom speedily died. Shortly the entire building was filled to its utmost capacity with wounded and sick from the front. From the city a large corps of volunteer nurses, mostly ladies, came in to wait upon the needy and administer comfort and consolation. How like angels they seemed, and how noble at last appeared the human face divine. Wonderful, the contrast between what I had seen in the camp and what met my gaze now. The expressions and phases of human nature seemed so different that relationship appeared almost impossible. Yet if these dear ladies were angels, as the men gratefully called them, the soldiers were their acknowledged brothers, and no attention or sacrifice seemed too much for their hands and their hearts. With great satisfaction I recall among these devoted helpers the family of Mr. John Welch, and several others, from whom I received attention in varied forms.

My eyes were receiving constant care and treatment, certainly of the most skillful kind; and I supposed they were becoming daily and hourly improved. One day Dr. Thomas called me to his office, and after a careful examination asked me how I was getting along. I told him I felt greatly encouraged, and thought I was doing well. Said he, "Take good care of your eyes, for I fear they will not last you long." This greatly shocked me, and I began to realize for almost the first time that possibly I might be blind. Dr. Hartshorn also called often to see me and to inquire after my condition. My eyes were often the topic of conversation and the subject of examination by physicians, but from the technical language used I could not learn their true condition.

I here witnessed many death-bed scenes, some of which have made life-long impressions on my mind. Some died amid the triumphs of faith, while others passed away in gloom and doubt. I sadly recall the death of a professed infidel. He had been often visited by Rev. Mr. P. and other clergymen; but he cared for none of their counsels, and regarded not their exhortations. He would even follow their departure with ravings and curses. But he sunk gradually, and finally died, as had been long evident to all he must. How horrible his death! Conscious up to almost the last moment, and seemingly convinced too late of his fatal mistake, he said, almost with dying breath, "I am a doomed and ruined man."

Soon after I came to the hospital I was appointed post-boy for the institution. To the city I went daily with the mail, and on other errands as desired. One day I obtained permission to visit Schuylkill Falls, and after performing my usual duties I took the steamer and went up the river. I spent most of the day pleasantly at the falls. On my return I fell in company with an old friend, a Mr. Grattz. We took a street-car together; and passing down Race Street, at the corner of Race and Twentieth I observed a large, fine building, and calling his attention to it inquired as to its object and use. He remarked that it was an institution for the blind. " Are the blind treated here?" I inquired. "No," said he, " they are educated here." For a moment I was overcome with the thought that I, yet, would be educated there as a blind man. In vain I strove to banish what seemed to me more a voice of prophecy than a mere thought of the excited imagination—years after I might come this way again; time would show.

One would have supposed that the experience of

a few months past would have sufficed to entirely
reform my life. The harrowing scenes of the hospital had destroyed my love for card-playing; and
though others amid those daily scenes of death
found pleasure therein, yet I had quit the habit.
Profanity, too, had ceased to be a common habit,
although not entirely relinquished. In moments
of anger I would lift my voice against the Almighty who had given me life and preserved my
being.

Returning to the hospital one evening, I learned
that Lieutenant McCoy had been there from our
regiment, gathering up recruits. He asked for
me; and I was greatly disappointed that I had not
been there to see him, and thus arrange for my return. I had by no means relinquished the idea of
returning to the field again. Moreover, I thought
myself sufficiently recovered to enter the service
at once for my usual duty. I was tired of the
hospital, and anxious for my old companions
and the exciting scenes of army-life. But the
lieutenant had gone without me, which was plain
assurance that I was regarded as unfit for duty.
Very soon the doctor called me to his office and
said that he had sent for my descriptive list, preparatory to my discharge from the service; that
my eyes were very bad; that they were getting
worse daily, and would last me but a short time.

He had reported me to the lieutenant as unfit for further service. I was depressed at the assurance that I was to be discharged, and absolutely horrified at what the doctor said of my eyes. Of course my father's admonition came back to me once more; and now I regretted inteusely that I had not allowed myself to be persuaded by him, and obeyed his kind admonitions. A week passed, and my discharge papers came.

The thought of going home this time awakened no feelings of satisfaction. I could no longer be welcomed as a soldier, and I had no prospect of immediate returu. My eyes were seemingly improved in that they pained me now but little, and appeared not to be bad. I could, however, read only with difficulty, and after night I did not easily get about. On reaching home I did not acqnaint my folks with the true condition of my eyes, and studied in every way to conceal such knowledge from them. Home soon became a round of monotonous scenes, and the relish for home society too soon began to wear away. I longed to go forth once more into the busy, outside world. Its wonderful activity and excitement I had enjoyed, and I wished and determined to see more of it. The terrible thought that soon I might forever close my eyes upon nature determined me to act promptly, if not morally and profitably. This

9

constant uneasiness on my part was noticed by my parents, and greatly pained them. They had longed for my return, and thanked God that at last their roving boy was once more beneath their roof. Out of ten thousand dangers, led by a gracious Providence, I had come forth to them. With them I might have continued in peace and security, and given their aching hearts some relief if I had chosen. But no; I must go forth again, and thus bring new and fresh trouble to hearts already broken by my foolish and maddened career.

Without my knowledge, and hoping thereby to anchor me near by home, my father had secured for me a situation as clerk, in a store in Philadelphia. I was glad to go, and intended to give close attention to business. I was not, however, suited with my position, and found also much trouble in rendering the service required of me at night, from the dimness of my vision. I determined, therefore, at the end of one week to return home. With partial contentedness I continued with my parents now until toward spring, when with the return of warm weather I again became uneasy, and determined to see something of the world. Ocean life, as it had been pictured to me by the fancies of story-writers, came vividly back to me in all its golden colors, and I longed to be a sailor; not, however, so much for the duties of a

sailor's life as the constant changes it would bring
to my decaying vision. I hoped to ship to some
foreign port, and thus visit the nations of the Old
World.

I told my mother one day that I was going down
to Philadelphia. She supposing it to be my purpose to return to the store again, prepared me but
a change, with a few most needed things, for a
brief absence. In a short time, she thought, I would
be home again, and she would more generously provide for my wants. It was well that she was cheered by such a hope, and saw not the future with
its thick and gathering clouds. What a weight of
sorrow and anxiety is often piled upon a dear
mother's heart by a wayward son. Joy and gladness only should be borne to them from us. Heavy
hearts will they have even if love only be our of-
ferings

CHAPTER XXV.

WILD ADVENTURES.

On my way to Philadelphia I met an old school-
mate, who had been home on a brief furlough from
the front. He was now returning again to the
field for further duty. We went to the theater together that night, and spent the next day like foolish and fast young men. I now sought to obtain
a position among the vessels as cabin-boy. Old
sailors admonished me against accepting the dangers and privations of a sailor's life, and exchanging
home for its evils and toils. They knew of what
they spoke, and could have abundantly confirmed
all of their convictions from their personal experiences. But I was in no condition to accept
such advice. I *would* see the world, whatever the
dangers and privations that awaited me. Unmind-
ful of their warnings, I rambled on among the
vessels, but was rejected everywhere as unsuited
to the wants of all. Toward dark, weary and hungry, I felt like despairing, and was about to turn
away from the river, when I saw a large schooner

lying at Dock-Street wharf. I thought I would try once more. I saw no person on board, but heard voices from below, and so proceeded on deck. I descended to the cabin and saw about a dozen men, mostly drunk, and carousing over a large jug of rum. Gazing upon the scene in silence for a moment, I thought to turn away, for with the sight I was both shocked and disgusted. But I had no money left, had had no supper, and knew not where I could obtain a lodging. To go home was now out of the question, and I resolved, therefore, to accept any chance, with anybody and for any labor. I said, finally, "Is the captain of this vessel present?" In response to my inquiry I had pointed out to me a large, burly-looking fellow as the one who bore the honors of the position. "Do you wish a boy, captain?" "I wish a cook," said he. "I can cook," I replied, remembering that I had seen some service of that sort in the army. "If you will work for $12.00 per month, and give us plenty to eat, you can come aboard." "How soon can I come?" "In an hour, as we wish to sail." I soon returned with my bundle, and prepared supper for the crew to the best of my ability. All was satisfactory, as I supposed, as no fault was found. However, they were from their intoxication but poor judges at best.

A tug-boat now towed us down the river for

several miles, when the vessel set sail for her intended point. Preparing bread for the morning, I gladly retired for my rest. I found next day that poor bread was the result of my first effort in that line; and the captain showed his appreciation of my failure by tauntings and sharp reproofs. I had seen rough men before, but never such conduct as these men exhibited. I saw that I had made a great mistake in shipping with them, and would have been quite as well off in the streets of the city, a beggar for my bread. But it was too late to correct my mistake, and I must go forward and make the best of it. In my anxiety to board the vessel I had not even inquired its destination. Fortunately for me, its voyage was not to be extended. Its destination was Chesapeake Bay, and its object a cargo of oysters for the city. Fairly under way, we encountered a severe storm. The vessel sprung a leak, and several inches of water came into the cabin. I became very sea-sick, and somewhat terrified. I was ordered to work, as soon as able, in different parts of the ship, as I found time outside of my regular duties as cook. I made poor progress in the general labor, and was rewarded with almost constant curses. I found that the vessel was an old, abandoned ship, and wholly unfit for service.

The vessel finally made harbor safely, and we

tarried until the fury of the storm abated. When
Sabbath came I expected rest, but found that the
men took no account of it. I was shocked at this
desecration, for with all my roughness I had ever
sacredly observed this day. My Puritanical instructions had sanctified the day to me. The vessel was but partly loaded, when its leaky condition
admonished the men that they must desist and return as speedily as possible. We got safely to
within some fifteen miles of Phildelphia, when the
vessel-grounded, from the intoxicated condition of
the helmsman. I saw but little chance for immediate sailing; and I importuned the captain to pay
me off and put me ashore at Chester. He refused
to pay me anything before reaching Philadelphia,
but ordered two of his men to row me ashore.
When within fifty yards of the shore they, for the
supposed fun of the thing, dumped me into the
stream, left me to the mercy of the waves, and returned toward the ship. Being a good swimmer,
I finally made the shore, but in an exhausted condition. Some young men while bathing had noticed the entire action. Finding me penniless,
they took up a collection of a dollar, and I boarded the train for Philadelphia. On my arrival I
called on a Mr. Thornton, whom I knew to be interested in the ownership of the vessel, and told
him my story. He kindly paid me off, and hired

me to work in unloading the vessel on its arrival. Being badly treated by the wharf-boys, I remained but a week with him.

At this junction of affairs my father came for me, and pleaded with me to go home with him. I finally concluded to do so; but on the way to the depot he took occasion to reprove me for my general course and conduct. His criticisms were altogether just, and with the tenderness of a father; but my heart was altogether wrong, and I was in no condition for even gentle reproof. It was almost nothing to me that my mother was wasting her very life in mourning over my course. I could even add further weight to her grief, and burden her heart with yet greater sorrow. At a corner I dodged my father, and by running was soon out of his sight and beyond his reach. The poor, despairing man must now go back to his home alone, with only new evidence of my profligacy and unworthiness. What wonder if then his heart had steeled against me, and even if a mother's love had changed into the coolest indifference? But I knew that this could not be so. While my mother lived she would love her wayward son, and daily pray for his moral recovery and speedy return.

I now determined to sail again. I found a vessel going to Boston, and obtained the position of assistant cook. This was a large, fine schooner, belonging to Buxton, Maine. The captain was a perfect gentleman; and he and his wife showed me the kindest possible attention. We had a delightful trip to Boston, but nothing of interest and deserving special note occurred during its progress. The captain offered me constant employment and fair wages if I would remain on his vessel; but wishing to see Boston, I preferred to decline his offer and remain for a time in the city. After visiting Quincy Markets I found near by accommodations for board, at $5.00 per week. I hardly had enough to pay two weeks' board at these figures, and began to feel the want of clothing as well as boarding. My boarding-master, a Mr. Clark, showed me great kindness at first—a kindness that altogether surprised me. With him I visited Boston Commons, and tried to enlist. I was about being accepted, when the condition of my eyes being noticed in the last moment, I was rejected. He then tried to enlist me in the navy, representing me as an English orphan boy, lately arrived in this country. In this, however, he failed. Meantime my money was all gone, and I was in arrears for board some $20.00. My clothes were threadbare; and I complained to Mr. Clark of my appearance. He offered me an order on the tailor for a suit. This I declined to take; and he ac-

companied me personally to the merchaut's and
furnished me with an entire suit of navy clothes.
I was astonished, and asked him where his pay
was to come from. He said, "Never mind, now;
I will find something for you after a brief time."
He proposed that I ship as a sailor, which I readily consented to do, but feared I would be rejected
from inexperience.

And now another boy arrived at Mr. Clark's.
He had been there before. He was about my own
age, was very fast, and had spent a time for criminal misconduct in the tombs. Together we went
with Clark to the shipping offices, and inquired
for opportunities for shipping boys, but without
immediate results. The Fourth of July came; and
I thought myself in a delightful place to spend the
day, if I only had money. And to my happy surprise Clark, in the early morning, handed me a
five-dollar bill, insisting simply on my return at
five o'clock, as he had work for me. The wonderful fascinations of the day held me still later than
this; and when, about dark, I did return, I found
Mr. Clark very much out of humor, and received,
much as I deserved, a very severe reprimand. 'He
said he had a good job for me, but I had come too
late for it. A few days afterward he came to us
on Boston Commons, and said, "Come immediately; I have a job for you." We went with him to

the shipping-office, and he engaged in low conversation with a bloated fellow at the desk. This
stranger soon approached, complimenting us with,
"You will make fine sailors, my boys." At this
point a short, lean, gray-haired German, with sailor-
like manners, entered the office and said to Mr.
Clark, "Vell, you have de poys." "Yes," said
Mr. Clark, pointing to me; "here is a boy that can
take down a royal yard for you in the twinkling of
an eye." "Captain Sourbier," said Mr. Clark to
me. I advanced and shook hands with the captain, thinking, meanwhile, that his name sounded
quite as funny as he was himself in appearance.
"Have you ever peen to sea, my poy?" I said
yes, calling to mind my recent ventures. "Vell,
Mr. Clark, how much you vant for de poy?" They
advanced to the desk and engaged in an undertone
talk; and the captain paid over a sum of money
to the shipping master. At this transaction Mr.
Clark seemed pleased; and I began to understand
that there was business before me. My days of
leisure and city sight-seeing appeared, with this
new scene, to be about closing up; and I naturally
wished to understand somewhat further about the
transaction, inasmuch as I was a party deeply interested in the case. The captain, now drawing
near to me, said, "How long, my poy, have you
peen a sailor?" Mr. Clark gave me no time to

answer, but at once responded, "He has been on one voyage only." Several nautical questions were propounded, which, by Clark's help, I managed to answer. The captain, however, seemed satisfied, and said quite pleasantly, "Ven you be a good poy, I vill give you blenty money." In short, he would do for me anything and everything if I would be good; and he would also take me to his home in Germany.

I had made no inquiry of Mr. Clark as to the whereabouts of the vessel I was to sail in, nor its destination; and now everything was conducted so strangely that I was quite bewildered, and really supposed this would end very much like other attempts of the same sort. On inquiry, I found that Sourbier was both commander and proprietor of his vessel, a German trader, and that he was running between New York and South America. He was now bound for Rio Janeiro, Brazil; and from thence he intended returning to Germany.

Clark seemed very nervous and impatient during our conversation, and finally interrupted our talk with, "Come, we must go; here it is four o'clock." The captain said, as we arose to go, "Come mit de poys at five o'clock." "All right, captain," said Clark; "we will be on hand promptly." He took us directly to a sailor's furnishing store and said, "Now, boys, buy what you wish." I gazed

about for a moment, seeing everything conceivable
in the sailor's line.   Various kinds of clothing, and
every variety of utensils needed by a sailor, either
for his comfort or amusement, were there.   I said,
"I do not know what I want. Buy me what you
choose."   I knew, too, that I had no money with
which to make purchases.   Clark then said to the
clerk, "Put them each up a pair of hickories
[shirts], two pairs of pants, knife, pipe and tobacco, and throw them in a pair of dunkeries [over-
alls]."   A few minutes sufficed for this, and I went
to the house to give the folks good-by.   This made
me think of home; for however strange these trans-
actions were, the house of Clark had become a
home for me.   I was troubled intensely with my
thoughts of home; and the vision of my gray-
haired father and sorrowing mother came up dis-
turbingly to me.   I said to Clark, "You must give
me a few minutes in which to write to my folks.
Up to this time I had, to my shame, written them
nothing; neither had they, as I know of, heard
one word of me since I left my father at a street-
corner in Philadelphia.   I wrote my letter and
handed it to Clark, with the request that he post
it.   This service he promised; but as the letter never reached my father, I have no reason to believe
he ever performed it.   I wrote my father but a
few lines, telling him of my health· that I was

now in Boston, but expected to leave at once to be gone a good while; wishing them to be of good cheer, etc. I asked no response, as much as I wished to hear from home, as I knew not where I could receive a letter from them. Clark, in whose hands I now felt myself an unwilling prisoner, called on me to hurry up my writing and come on. We returned to the store, where a wagon was in waiting, by which, after a few minutes' drive, we reached the wharf, where we found a boat in waiting. This was manned by four burly oarsmen, who received us on board, and after our farewells to Clark rowed us out to the ship, a half mile distant.

CHAPTER XXVI.

A HOME ON THE DEEP.

Once upon the vessel, I fixed my eyes only on the receding boat, watching the progress of the oarsmen until they nearly reached the shore. Then, with heavy heart, I turned to inspect the ship, my future floating home. It was what is known as a bark, or a vessel with three masts, having her fore and main masts rigged as a ship, and her mizzen, or hind-mast sail, as a schooner. It was a goodly vessel, stoutly built, but old enough to show that she had passed through many a storm and had received their blackening signs.

Captain Sourbier was engaged in sweeping the deck, and in the enjoyment of his short-stemmed pipe seemed at first wholly unconscious of our arrival. The crew, which consisted of some dozen or fifteen men, were lounging about the ship as though they, instead of the captain, were her proprietors. I was not pleased at all, either with the general appearance of things or with the men. I determined, in my tracks, that if ever opportunity

should offer I would steal away from such a place
as that. Thoughts of the dear home I had left so
foolishly, that I might realize the glory of ocean-
life, but increased this determination within me.
Still, the impossibility of escape seemed absolute,
and I felt that at once I might as well banish such
a notion from my mind.   At last the captain threw
down his broom and called to the mate, with whom
he exchanged some words in German. The mate
smilingly called us and bid us follow him. He
led the way to the forecastle, the part of the vessel where the sailors live. Pointing to the companion way, he told us to go below and put away
our goods. Here we found the roughest and fil-
thiest looking place I was ever in. A short, flabby
Dutchman sat on a chest mending his torn and
well-worn pants. This was the cook of the vessel.
He pointed out to us our berths, in which we put
our clothing. After a word of further conversation with this fellow, we went above again to the
deck. The fat German from below, however, followed us up, and insisted on further conversation.
"Vat for you come on a German ship? You no
speak German." Noticing a large lot of cabbage,
turnips, beef, etc., near the galley, or ship's kitch-
en, I said, "I guess we will get along well with the
Germans; I see you live pretty well." Laughing,
he said, "You like dot stuff? Ve not get so good

eat by aud by. You like peans?" "Yes," said I,
"I became very fond of them while in the army."

The captain approaching, the cook retired to
the galley for his dnties. The captain was armed
with a heavy broom, and as he approached he said,
"You got notings to do, hey? You come mit
me, I'll giff you somedings." He put us to sweeping the deck, which was already clean from the
sweeping of others. Dan, my mate, was evidently homesick already; and he said to me as we began to sweep, "Jimmy, I don't like this old Dutchman. What do you think of him?" He waited
not for my opinion, which, if expressed, would
have been in perfect accord with his own. "Let
us go ashore," said Dan. "What for, and how?"
said I. "We'll tell the captain that we have no
oil-skins, and he will let us have the boat to go
for them." This, I well knew, was presuming too
much, for our Dutch captain was not altogether
dumb. These oil-skins were needed as protections
from the storm, and we should have had them.
They were to be mentioned, however, only as a pre-
text. We knew we had no money with which to
buy them if we were ashore. Advancing to the
captain we told him our wish, but were met, of
course, with his flat and angry refusal. He doubtless knew what we wanted as well as we ourselves.
Dan showed his rage, and told the captain to keep

10

his boat, saying to me aside that he would go ashore
when he wanted to. Returning to the forecastle,
the cook laughed heartily and tauntingly at our
expense and confusion. He had overheard the
conversation, and had enjoyed our rebuff.

Supper was now announced; but it was too coarse
and unpalatable for relishing, and I could eat hardly anything. I now saw but too plainly that I had
been fearfully imposed upon, and began to fear for
the future. I thought again of my father's admonitions, and of his pale, care-worn face. I
wished now for my mother's table and the sweet
tokens of her love. But home was far away, and
voluntarily and cruelly I had wandered from it.
I was the only guilty one; and I would have
thanked God could I have known that I was the
only suffering one. Other hearts, however, were
bleeding besides my own; and those hearts were
beating in perfect innocence

The lights of the city were now flashing and
flickering in the distance; and while I was wishing myself once more upon solid ground, and amid
their pleasant blaze, the mate's voice attracted my
attention. He directed me to take my turn on
watch, and told Dan to go below. I hardly knew
the nature of the duty required, but knew well
enough that no sleep would be allowed. I prepared, therefore, for wakeful work by going be-

low for tobacco and pipe. Thus armed, I proceeded to the forcastle, when I was directed to keep a
sharp lookout. Lighting my pipe, I began my
pacing and my smoking. Most of the sailors had
retired, a few only remaining above, humming
their old German tunes. A little later Dan came
to my side silently and said, "Jimmy, I shall not
stay in this old box. This crew is wicked enough
to eat a fellow." I had began to think as much,
but refrained just then from any confirmation of
his views. "Had I known this vessel," I said, "I
would never have come aboard of her." "Old
Clark," said he, "is a villain. He is mean enough
to send a fellow anywhere, if he can make a dollar
by it." With me the proceedings of the past twen-
ty-four hours had seemed very mysterious, and
withal darkly underhanded. Evidently he was relieved at my going, which I could explain on no
principle of professed friendship. His course had
been strange, and I wholly misunderstood it.
"How much advance pay did he get out of you?"
Dan asked. "Advance?" said I, "what do you
mean?" "How much pay did the shipper give
him for you?" This was all news to me; and now
it came to my mind at once that Clark had kept
and shipped me wholly as a matter of personal
profit. Had he enlisted me, as he first hoped, he
would have obtained a bounty and advance pay at

my expense; and now, as it afterward proved, he had received two months' pay, having shipped me at $25.00 per month.

I now awakened to the fact that I was sold, literally, to a service for which I had no qualification, and of which I knew absolutely nothing. I, too, had been a party to the deception of the captain, that I might please Clark, whom I had taken for a friend. I had bound my own hands with chains of more than steel; and I was to pay but too dearly for all the benefits I had gained from a supposed friend. I dreaded the wrath of Captain Sourbier when he should come to learn that I was inexperienced, and partially blind as well. It was a grand imposition on him, and one for which I was grossly guilty myself.

"But," said Dan, "I am determined to get out of this." "How can you?" said I. "The captain will not let you have the boat." "Never mind," said he, "I will fix that. The question is, Will you go with me? Clark has *shanghaied* you into this service." He then detailed to me his plan of escape. The captain's gig, or light boat, was dangling loosely from the cranes on the quarter-deck. It was only necessary to let go the halyards and drop the boat into the water. This would create some noise; but he had a remedy against that. Dan proposed to loosen the boat after all became quiet. He was sure we could reach the shore in safety; and then we would quickly leave the city. The captain was sleeping so near by that I was sure he would hear the falling of the boat, and that any attempt at escape would cost us our lives. I wished to leave the ship most heartily, and thus get back home again; but rather than run the chances of losing life, I would prefer to stay aboard the ship. But Dan was determined not to be put off by my lack of courage and indecision. Would I not go, he would take the chances alone. So, bidding me good-night, he went below, and I continued my pacing and my smoking.

All was quiet, save the splash of the policemens' boat-oars as they passed up and down the harbor. I had fallen into an almost unconscious reverie, when I was aroused by the signal of eight bells, struck for the change of the watch. The mate, coming on deck, directed me to go below and call Dan. This I did; and leaving him and the mate on deck I went down to my berth for sleep, but most truly with a heavy heart. Before the morn I was aroused by the call of all hands to deck. I arose hastily, went above, and found eight or ten men at the windlass. It was still pitchy dark. I was told to heave with the rest. The night-air was made to ring with the singing of the men, commingled with the noisy clanking of the rusty chain as it came up from the deep, dark see below. I longed for the daylight, as I had to feel my way around, and feared every moment I should be told to do something which I could not do for the darkness. Where was Dan, I wondered. He is not at the windlass, and I have seen no sight of him since rising. Has he indeed made good his threatening vow, and left the ship under the cover of the night? Am I indeed alone amid this ship's awful crew? To me, strange as it may seem, Dan was a companion to whom my very heart went out, especially since the broad sea had received us from the native land.

But my reverie was suddenly interrupted by the cry of the captain, in sharp German accents, to which the men responded with a will, moving toward the stern of the vessel. I tried to follow, but stumbled over the ropes several times before reaching the rallying center of the men—the vessel's stern. The most of the men were soon aloft, loosening the sails, while I was holding by the shroud, fearing I should fall. The mate now seized me, and told me to go aloft and loosen the royal, the top-sail at the head of the top-gallant-sail. I knew full well the dizzy hight of its position, and yet I dared not refuse. Many of the heavy men never ventured to loosen this sail. I climbed to the half-moon, but about one third of the distance, and feared to go farther. Here I sat down and began to cry, neither daring to go forward or back to the deck. I heard the voice of the captain calling repeatedly for the boy; but I ventured no answer. I could hear the angry voices of the men about me, jabbering in German, with frequent oaths interspersing their words; but for the darkness and the dimness of my vision I could descry no man in the rigging. The mate soon passed me without the sign of a recognition; but, swearing about the boy and the royal, he wended his way upward to loosen it himself. Once above me, I took advantage of his distance to climb down again upon the deck. The captain met me, muttering something most angrily; but in my defense I told him I was sick. He was not, however, in a mood to let me off, but set me to coiling rope, a work at which, from the darkness, I made but poor progress.

Soon, to my relief, the gray light of the morning broke upon us; and a brisk breeze, I saw, was speedily carrying us seaward. How well I remember the splashing of the waves, and the deep gurgling of the water as we plowed our way through the sea. Again I began to wonder where Dan was, when the captain and mate angrily approached me and addressed the same question to me, "Where is dat oder fellow?" "Below, I suppose," said I.

"You know where he is," the captain retorted; "what for you lie?" His menacing position before me made me fear he would fell me with a maddened blow. In fear, I walked away, and the captain followed me to the forcastle. He took Dan's wardrobe from his berth; and after examining it carefully, as if he expected to find some signs of Dan within it, he carried it to his own quarters. If he could not have the boy, he would make the best use of the boy's apparel. Dan's flight and the method of his procedure were now well understood by all, and was the topic of excited conversation for the day. Although I could understand but little, I knew that a spirit of boasting vengeance was being nursed against poor Dan; and in my heart I was glad that several hours' sail had separated him and them before his leave-taking had been noticed. It certainly was a good thing for him, as he might, if caught, have tested the virtue of hemp and the strength of the yard-arm.

I spent the day in coiling rope, sweeping deck, etc., as best I could. Meanwhile I wondered what I had best do to make my situation as comfortable as possible. Should I tell the captain the actual condition of things, or should I defer the matter until a more favorable opportunity? But I had not sufficient courage to own the truth, and so deferred action for the time. Night came on again, and I was put upon the watch, as the night before. An excellent watch, thought I—a poor, blind boy, who could not descry a passing vessel if but a ship's length away! Surely *I* will do to take down a top-sail-yard, Captain Sourbier! Oh, that I had gone with lucky Dan. By this time, thought I, he is looking about for another ship.

The watch-hours wore away without special incident, and I passed down to my berth for rest again. With early dawn I was called once more on deck. Stretched around me was a magnificent expanse of blue. No land could be descried in any direction. For the first time I had lost sight of the solid earth. I was resting upon the billowy bosom of the mighty deep; and yet I felt that with all my sins I was in the hollow of God's own hand. The vast ocean appeared to me like one wonderful waste of water. Of what utility, thought I, is this wonderful waste to man? Why so large a portion of the globe but billowy water, which no man can cultivate, and whereon men can not permanently live? It is not mere scenery for the eye, for from the shore, but its narrowest rim can be taken into the field of wondering vision. The ocean covers three fifths of that globe which God gave to man for his own home. How unnatural seems this division. How strange, at least at first thought, it had not been reversed. And yet

we must admit that this, with all God's other
works, is both right and best. The ocean as it is,
is of the greatest conceivable importance to man,
and essential, it is claimed, to the general grand
harmony of the laws of nature. It is the grand
highway of all nations, built by God, the Supreme
Architect, for the commerce of the world. It is
worth more than a thousand railroads running between America and Europe or Africa, and one over
which the world may pass without let or hinder-
ance. The products of the most distant climes
may be borne upon its bosom; and thus the distant
regions of the earth will be made to contribute of
their bounties to the common table of a race. Countries are widely separated from each other, and
thus allowed to grow up in measurable independence of each, and train their peoples in their
mutually dissimilar habits and methods. These
widely separated schools are doubtless to the general advantage of the nations, and but add to the
intellectual fruitfulness of the world. The ocean,
too, is a barrier impassable to the barbarian, one
over which he can not pass in his frail canoe, nor
at all, indeed, until he consents to adopt the modes
and habits of civilization. The sea, literally, con-
stitutes the empire of civilization, whatever may
be said of some portions of the earth. The barbarian may scale the mountain, penetrate the for-

est, and hold his own sway over the vale and the plain, but the sea he must relinquish to the stronger rule of the civilized races. And old ocean, too, is the great store-house of rain, where Nature distills her genial drops that make glad the earth and fruitful the field. For this purpose the annual evaporation of all the oceans is supposed to equal a depth of about fourteen feet; that is, if the oceans did not receive any rain during the year, nor any supply from the rivers of the world, they would fall in depth fourteen feet during that time. The moisture needed by the earth could perhaps be supplied with a sea-surface no less than that we have.

And then I thought of the depth of these vast waters, upon the bosom of which I was sailing out from my native clime and home. As the mountain tops are above the valley, so are the deep vales of the sea below the surface of the waters thereof. What a wondrous depth beneath me, and how deep would be my grave if I should lie down here in death. LaPlace estimates the average depth of the ocean at ten miles, while the higher mountains are little more than five miles in elevation. The greatest ascertained depth of the Atlantic is about five miles, while the Pacific is considered deeper than the Atlantic.

Soon after rising I witnessed the magnificent sunrise of the sea, a scene before which the world with its most fastidious taste might proudly stand entranced. I had never before witnessed anything of such real glory. I had seen the king of day as he had come up from the beautiful plain, as though rising from his grave of verdure, and I had seen his smiling face rising majestically above the mountain-top, as if like a monarch, to look down from the world's higher throne upon the waking multitudes of earth; but such grandeur as a clear sunrise at sea I had never witnessed or imagined. No pen can paint the scene; and for once even bold imagination finds herself baffled in the endeavor. It rose as a smiling beauty, and shone like the face of God, which it sweetly represented. What wonder that this king of day, this source of heat and light and even life, has been mistaken for God himself, and worshiped as such! If ever I felt like yielding reverence and bestowing worship before the shrine of the sun it was now. Rising as from the deep blue sea, it seemed as if coming forth from its nightly immersion, perfectly cleansed from every stain, while every ray appeared to offer proof of its own complete innocence. From the beautiful glory left in its wake, one would suppose with Shakespeare that it had been "bathing in fiery floods." Truly, for once the Spirit of God seemed to move upon the face of the waters before my own eyes. At the very rising of the sun millions of briny drops abandon their mighty ocean-cradle, and, unseen to mortal eye, rise upward into the upper blue, to form silvery clouds from which God may fashion the refreshing shower. The very waves seem newly mad with joy as they dance and flash in the sunlight, covering the sea with one broad, golden luster.

If in the wide world anything which I have seen equals or comes nearly in approach to the sunrise of the sea, it is its own opposite image—the sunset of the sea. The description of this I shall not trust to my own pen, but shall, with passing, breathe upon the reader the words of the poet in brief

"Now the sun lay low in the golden West,
With bars of purple across his breast.

"The skies were aflame with the sunset's glow;
The billows were all aflame below;

'The far horizon seemed the gate
To some mystic world's enchanted state.

"And all the air was a luminous mist,
Crimson, and amber, and amethyst."
—*Mrs. Julia C. R. Dorr.*

And again the poet Millard aids and refreshes my thought with his song:

"I've seen, behind the ocean wave,
The sun his golden pinions lave,
Still sending o'er the watery way
The milder beams of closing day;

The sky above, like burnished gold,
Reflected on each wave that rolled,
While far as eye could trace the scene
The sea was clad in dazzling sheen;
Above, around, a halo spread,
Till glory mantled ocean-bed.

"Bright scene of mild departing day,
I love to while an hour away
In gazing on thy fading light,
And watch the gath'ring shades of night.
On the ship's deck how oft I've stood
And eyed thy glory o'er the flood,
Till faintly and more faintly glowed
The golden beauties thou hadst strewed;
Till night its somber pall had spread,
And Luna shone in Phœbus' stead."

CHAPTER XXVII.

LIFE ON THE SEA.

For several hours I was made to work with others of the crew at repairing the well-worn sails.
The captain, meanwhile, was closely eyeing me
from the wheel, and I was quite sure that he was
by no means pleased with the progress I was making. A shrill whistle caused me to look toward
him, when he beckoned me to his side. He told
me to take the wheel and steer the ship. This, in
calm weather, was but a pleasant service; and
could I have distinctly seen, as the work required, I should have cared for nothing better. I
took the wheel, as I was bid, and observed the
course I was to follow. The compass was in the
binnacle-box, but a short distance from me, and
yet I could so indistinctly see the points of the
compass that I soon had the ship aback. This,
of course, brought the captain to my side in a terrible rage. With an oath, he dragged me from
the wheel and righted the ship; and then, leaving
me once more, he charged me to mind well my

business. Soon, however, in spite of my best en-
endeavors, the ship was thrown aback worse than
before. This time he came fiercely upon me, and
gave me a blow the sting of which I felt for a long
time. He then demanded to know, and quite reasonably, too, why I did not keep her on her right
course. I now confessed to him the fact that I
could not see. Again, with an oath, he struck
me, asking why, then, I had come aboard his ship.
The captain was brutal; but it is the part of hon-
or in me to confess that he had some show of reason for his brutality. He, in good faith, had hired
me for a special service, and I had given him ample assurance that I was able to perform all he
should ask. I had sought to dupe him, but had
to a worse extent foolishly duped myself, to please
Mr. Clark, the Boston villain, into whose hands I
had fallen. But God, perhaps, was punishing me
in part for my guilty conduct toward parents whose
hearts had ever shown me purest love. Did I suffer much, it was only less than I righteously deserved; and possibly this mode of punishment was
God's method for the correction of my life.

Another was now called to the wheel, and the
captain put me on other duty. Days now passed
with unvarying monotony, but bringing to my
broken and disconsolate soul daily reproofs, kicks,
and curses from the mate and captain, and frequent

stinging insults from the men. My inexperience
made me the butt of ridicule with them, which
they were less willing to excuse from my former
professions of knowledge in the sea-going line.
They often treated me with derision and contempt,
the old German cook, in whom I had hoped to
find a friend, freely joining with the rest. Cloudy
weather and a brisk sea soon made the ocean rough,
and I began to feel, for the first time, sensations of
nausea. Coming upon the deck, I was greeted
with a cloud of spray which wet me to the skin.
It was blowing a stiff breeze, and I was unable to
keep my feet, much to the merriment of the sailors. In essaying to go to the after-part of the
deck I sought to make the distance before the
ship should lurch again, and therefore ran. But
this special endeavor was all against me. My
haste, combined with the lurching of the vessel,
threw me repeatedly to the opposite side of the
ship, and entirely out of my line of direction. This
effort on my part occasioned loud bursts of laughter
from the men. The violent agitation, also, soon
told severely on me, and I speedily began to experience the horrors of sea-sickness. I had fain
hoped that I had passed beyond the danger of this
species of miserable suffering. It came, however,
at last, and I was to know it in its worst and most
terrible form.

11

Of some of the crew I asked a remedy for my trouble, but they only answered me with their derisive laughter. I had somewhere read or heard that salt-water was a remedy for the disease, and so I drank plentifully of it, hoping thereby to obtain relief. This, of course, but added to my trouble and distress. The old cook had been, he had told me, a sailor from a boy. Surely he would know what to do for my relief, and in such an hour would show me pity. I staggered toward the galley. "Vat you vant," he said, as I came in the door. "I am sick," said I; "dreadfully sick. Can you not give me something for my relief?" "I gives you someding vat makes you right avay petter. You like some dinner? Ve got peans for dinner." The thought of dinner but disgusted · me, of course. He left the galley, as I supposed, for the purpose of getting something for my relief. He soon returned, followed by the loud shouts of the men and their now torturing presence. Hoping he brought relief, I quickly answered to his call to come forth from the galley. He bid me open my mouth, and presented to me a piece of fat pork tied by a long string, which he held. This he wished me to swallow. Loud laughter from the surrounding crowd was the reward of his ungenerous proposition. This was more than I could bear and I burst into tears and gladly went from their presence. At the dinner one of the crew who professed some measure of friendship induced me to eat of bean-soup. This I did, in my hunger, hoping for some relief; but it only made me worse than ever.

Finally the wind subsided, the weather modified, the sea became quite calm, and I began to recover from my horrible sickness. I had experienced in this sickness what many have tried but none have ever been able to describe. The very agonies of death could hardly be worse; and yet with all its horrors the sickness is seldom, if ever, fatal. Perhaps there is no actual preventive known, and no cure when once its agonies are upon one. Precautions can be taken, however, which will lessen its fury, and conditions observed which will ease the patient. Lord Byron quotes his friend Dr. Granville as saying that the true way to escape the malady is to take, on starting, forty-five drops of laudanum, and further doses as often afterward as uneasiness occurs. In his Don Juan he gives a comical description of the disease; but it is not suited to these pages. The conduct of the crew toward me wholly quenched any fire of love or respect that may have glowed upon the altar of my heart for them. I determined never again to trouble them with my wants, or even ask of them a favor.

My appetite was now voracious; but the fresh

provisions of the ship were wholly exhausted, and I began to realize that on board a German ship there was little good eating, as the old cook had forewarned me. Wormy sea-biscuit, meat unfit to eat, beans, and corn-coffee innocent of sugar, made up the round of our daily diet. For such stuff I had little relish ; and yet I must eat of this or starve. The captain, meantime, fared better and well enough. The steward prepared for him his daily ham and eggs, with pure coffee, sugar, and other luxuries. Even his Newfoundland dog was furnished with a plate and his slice of ham. Several sheep had been put aboard for his supply; and eggs were furnished by a brood of fine fowl. By close watching I obtained occasionally a fresh egg, which I relished better than he did his daily, dainty wine; and then a few times I managed to get the leavings of his own meals, intercepting what was intended for the Newfoundland's plate, from the kitchen.

On board our vessel were three passengers, to whose presence, it is highly probable, I owe even life itself. The bitterness of my cup was more than once sweetened by kindly looks and genial words. These passengers consisted of a boy from Massachusetts, visiting an uncle in South America, an invalid gentleman voyaging simply for health, and, chief to me, a Mr. Watson, a merchant of New York. He was a well-proportioned, fine-looking

man, of much polish and very genial spirit. He
showed me a special friendship, for which I would
record my obligation with tears of grateful love
and recollection. As a rule, passengers were not
allowed the privilege of conversation with the crew;
but it so happened that I got many opportunities
therefor with Mr. Watson. From the first I noticed that he kindly watched me in my harsh treatment; and I knew that I could not mistake the
pity of his eye. The passengers spent their time
in taking observations, fishing, and gathering curi-
osities of general interest. Mr. Watson took his
daily bath, in a large tub in the forepart of the vessel; and this I daily filled for the bather, and also
waited upon him at such times as desired. Thus
I had frequent interviews with him. He kindly
inquired into my family and general history, which
I gladly gave him, with special particularity. As
time drew on my respect ripened into love for the
gentleman, and I knew I could count with certainty on his friendship. I took great comfort in the
thought that I had the kindly love of one being
on board the vessel. Yet there was much in store
for me in the way of wrathful treatment.

One day the captain was ordering the men to do
many things which I thought, under the circumstances, entirely unnecessary. Everything loose
about the vessel was being well secured. The ex-

tra spars were made doubly sure in their places, the top-sails were double reefed, and the royal that I had been expected to take down was loosened by another hand. The captain's eye was anxious'y and steadily fixed upon the sky. I soon learned that I was to have a new experience, one which, luckily, I had so far been spared. A storm was approaching; and the signs thereof were numerous, and had not escaped the vigilant eye of Captain Sourbier. The portents of this gathering storm did not appear to me as they would not to any unpracticed eye. The breeze began to freshen; and the white crest upon the blue-tongued waves was doubly grand and surpassingly beautiful to the curious eye.

Speaking of a white squall, Wm. Makepiece Thackery thus poetizes:

> "In our jovial, floating prison
> There was sleep from fore to mizzen,
> And never a star had risen
> The hazy sky to speck.
> Strange company we harbored;
> We'd a hundred Jews to larboard,
> Unwashed, uncombed, unbarbered—
> Jews black and brown and gray.
>
> *   *   *   *   *   *   *   *
>
> And so the hours kept tolling,
> And through the ocean rolling
> Went the brave Iberia, bowling,
> Before the break of day.

"When a squall, upon a sudden,
　　Came o'er the waters scudding;
　　And the clouds began to gather,
　　And the sea was lashed to lather,
　　And the lowering thunder grumbled,
　　And the lightning jumped and tumbled;
　　And the ship and all the ocean
　　Woke up in wild commotion;
　　And the cordage and the tackle
　　Began to shriek and crackle;
　　And the spray dashed o'er the funnels,
　　And down the deck, in runnels,
　　While the passengers awaken,
　　Most pityfully shaken."

R. Brown also thus describes a storm on Galli-
lee :

"Our bark was riding merrily,
　　A speck upon that summer sea;
　　But deep and hollow murmurs came,
　　That heralded the tempest waking,
　　The gathering cloud and flickering flame,
　　And thunders in the distance breaking;
　　The storm's first drops and fitful freeze,
　　That curled the bosom of the seas.

"And wild and high the hillows rose,
　　Fearful in strength and proudly foaming,
　　Starting like maniacs from repose,
　　Or dark and heartless plunderers, roaming.

But the poet-pen must fail to bring up the awful
beauty and fury of the storm at sea to the eye of
my reader. Once beheld, however, the scene re-
mains forever photographed within the deep cham-

bers of the soul. To witness its fury and feel its power, one may not stand a spectator upon the sheltered bank or commanding mountain; but he must be amid its roar and flash and horrid whirl. A brave heart must beat in that bosom which can behold the scene unmoved, and a heart of cold indifference that before such awful power will refuse to submit and soften into tenderness.

The flying-fish presented a magnificent sight preceding the rising storm. This fish is a fine specimen of the fruitful and varied life of the sea. It has a scaly head. Its mouth is without teeth, and its jaws are connected on each side. It is about fourteen inches in length, while its pectoral fins, which serve it as wings, are of great strength, and about three fourths the length of its body. It will often quit the water, rising about three feet, and fly a distance of two hundred and fifty to three hundred feet. It is then obliged to drop into the water again to moisten its fins, which in its progress become both dry and hard. This fish is the prey of the *dorado* under the water, and above it is pursued by the gull or albatross; and often, too, in escaping the one it is destroyed by the other. Its air-bladder is extremely large, and this greatly assists it in its aerial progress. Sometimes, as the vessel dips toward the sea, they attempt, if possible, to fly across the ship, and in great numbers drop upon the deck, where they flounder until returned again to the sea by the crew. They are undesirable for food, and hence their presence on deck is attended with no profit to the sailor.

A school of dolphins sporting about a vessel is a sight not altogether devoid of interest, while also a school of porpoises receives more than a passing notice. The dolphin is unusually playful before boisterous weather; aud in his uncouth gambols he seems happy that the storm is coming on. His measurement reaches occasionally a length of ten feet. He pursues and attacks small fish, but has also no fear of the whale. They have been seen firmly adhering to whales as those monsters have jumped out of the sea. The ancients possessed for this animal a wonderful and superstitious attachment; and illustrative of its affection they have recorded numerous anecdotes. They claimed it to have a rapturous fondness for music also; but their descriptions are more fanciful than correct.

The porpoise is smaller than the dolphin, being about six feet in length. It obtains its prey by swimming, and also, in shallow water, by rooting in the mud and sand like a hog. For this reason they are sometimes called by sailors seahogs. They were once regarded as great delicacies for the table, and were served to nobles, and even kings; but now, as food they are wholly dis-

carded. They will often jump from the water and
dive again, head-foremost, splashing the sea with
their tails. Their presence serves to break the
monotony of the sea; and in their sports they are
not altogether unattractive.

My condition was now pretty generally understood by both the captain and the crew; and it
gave me special relief in the direction of duty, I
being called on usually to do only what I was in
my condition well qualified for. The spirit of the
men toward me was also materially changed. Not
now essaying to do what I could not do, I was no
longer subject to their jeering and ridicule. To
some degree they showed me kindness and pity,
for which expressions I began to entertain feelings
of tender regard and cordial respect. My duties
were now wholly of the day, and consisted of rope-
coiling, deck-sweeping, tarring yarn for sail-mend-
ing, whipping the ropes to prevent their raveling,
and other light and generally pleasant duties.

For several days a very large, strange-looking
monster had been following and swimming close
by our ship, the nature of which was unknown to
our crew; and the captain, even, declared that he
had never seen anything resembling it. It was dark,
and spotted; and about six feet of its body we could
see almost constantly above the water. The captain finally determined to secure it, and for this

purpose about seventy-five fathoms of rope were coiled for use. The captain, descending over the starboard, struck the harpoon into the monster, when it instantly darted seaward with lightning speed. Unfortunately the steward, in crossing the ship, became entangled in the ropes and was dragged by the leg several feet. He would certainly have been hauled overboard had not the carpenter, who happened to stand near with hatchet in hand, severed the rope with a well-directed blow. By this means we lost our strange fish; but we all felt that with the loss a terrible fatality had been prevented. As it was, the leg of the steward was severely bruised; and for several days he could hobble about only with difficulty.

And now ensued what sailors dread even more than the storm—a deep, monotonous calm. To the steamer it is no objection in ocean-life, but a very special advantage. To a sailing-ship, however, whose only dependence is its sails, and therewith the driving winds of heaven, a calm is dreaded beyond possible expression. The weather-vane on the ship's quarter at such times is motionless; and a more delicate test sometimes resorted to by sailors to detect the least breath of sea-breeze, namely, that of casting a coal of fire into the sea, will often result in simply a perpendicular ascension of steam into the motionless air. Sometimes

for weeks the ship will lie without making any
progress, and meantime the sailors become exceedingly nervous and anxious. The least increased
motion of the sea is hailed with delight as the
hoped harbinger of the coming breeze. "The rays
of the sun are burning rays, while the deck be-
comes hot to the feet; the melting pitch boils up
from the seams, tar drops continually from the
rigging, the masts and booms display gaping cracks,
the flukes of the anchors are too hot to touch with
impunity," while no cloud shelters from the fierce
and fiery heat of the king of day.

Coleridge, in his "Ancient Mariner," thus briefly
describes the condition of the sea during a calm:

> "The sun came up upon the left,
>   Out of the sea came he;
> And he shone bright, and on the right
>   Went down into the sea.
>
> "Down dropped the breeze, the sails dropped down,
>   'Twas sad as sad could be ;
> And we did not speak, only to break
>   The silence of the sea.
>
> "Day after day, day after day
>   We stuck; nor breath, nor motion ;
> As idle as a painted ship
>   Upon a painted ocean."

M. Schele De Vere, author of "Stray Leaves
from the Book of Nature," thus discourses on the
"calm at sea:"

"Only when the wind is lulled and a calm has soothed the angry waves can the ocean be seen in its quiet majesty. But the aspect is apt to be dreary and lonely, whether we see the dark waves of the sea draw lazily in and out of rocky cliffs, or watch wearily the sea's perpetual swing, the melancholy wash of the endless waves. Away from the land, there is nothing so full of awe and horror as a perfectly calm sea. Man is spell-bound; a magic charm seems to chain him to the glassy and transparent waters; he can not move from the fatal spot, and death, slow, fearful, certain death, stares him in the face. He trembles as his despairing gaze meets the upturned, leaden eye of the shark, patiently waiting for him; as he hears far below the sigh of some grim monster, slowly shifting on his uneasy pillow of brine. Fancy knows but one picture more dreadful yet than tempest, shipwreck, or the burning of a vessel out at sea; it is a ship on the great ocean in a calm, with no hope for a breeze. On the same sunshine, on the same waves, the poor mariners gaze day by day with languid eye, even until the heart is sick and the body perishes."

Of course, here we have a description of an extended and fatal calm. The calm with us lasted some days, perhaps less than a week, when our hearts were made glad again by the rising breeze and the slow moving of our goodly ship.

CHAPTER XXVII.

OVER THE LINE AND INTO PORT.

We were now approaching the line, as the sailors pleased to call the equator. This is an imaginary line, belting the globe east and west, at a point equidistant from the north and south poles. At this line the inhabitants have days and nights of equal length the year around. The city of Quito, Ecuador, and the mouth of the river Amazon, in Brazil, are on the west and east ends of this line respectively, in South America, or at a point equally distant from the northern and southern poles. Among the sailors there was much talk of the *line;* and I half imagined that when I came to it, it would be visible to the eye. I was actually and yet half unconsciously on the watch for it. The tropical rains were almost constant, which made this part of our ocean-life exceedingly disagreeable; and yet the heat was so intense that we gladly consented to this heavy veiling of the sun and this constant weeping of nature. With a

clear sky we could, seemingly, have hardly endured the scalding heat of the day.

One evening the mate called me to the wheel,
and directed me to steer the ship. This was now
a work very rare, and I reluctantly took the wheel;
but the mate said he would be absent only a moment, and would keep an eye on the vessel. He
soon returned, and for an hour, until the shades of
evening began to deepen, we were engaged in
pleasant conversation. Neptune and the line had
well-nigh been forgotten by me, and I supposed
we were passed over and done with them. The
carpenter, I noticed, was busily engaged in unrav-
elling rope and working upon canvas in a manner
entirely strange, and which greatly puzzled me.
While I was wondering what his strange motions
could mean, and what interest his work could answer, I was startled by a sepulchral voice from the
forepart of the ship, crying out, "Ship, ahoy!
What vessel is this? Where is she bound?" and
numerous other questions, to which the mate, standing by me, responded pleasantly, and with no exhibition of emotion. During the time, I was peer-
ing into the darkness seaward, hoping to descry
some vessel, whence I supposed the voice to
proceed, and which I concluded was very near us.
" What vessel does the man speak from?" I inquired of the mate. "It is Neptune that is speaking

to us, said he." This character now climbed over
the bows of the vessel as if coming up out of the
sea, and stood upon the forecastle of the ship. He
was bellowing unceasingly, and in a jargon of
sounds almost unintelligible to me. The mate at
the wheel was now relieved, and went toward the
forecastle, directing me to follow him. Neptune,
as we advanced, came down from the deck and approached us, the mate giving me an introduction
to him as he came up. He had on his head something similar to a dunce-cap of immense proportions. He wore a long beard of manilla rope, and
his hair, which was of the same material, reached
down to his shoulders. He wore a large tunic,
which covered him to his ankles; and this was secured by a huge belt about him, which contained
a ponderous wooden knife, some two feet in length.
In one hand he carried a large harpoon partly covered with canvas, and in the other a large bucket
containing a mixture of tar, soap, and water, very
thick. Neptune then asked me about my sea-life.
He said it was his business to look up green sea-
men who had never crossed the line, and among
the rest it was his duty to shave them. I naturally
and with horror now cast my eyes down into the
thick black lather of his bucket; but in an instant
he roughly grabbed me, pulled off my hat, and
seated me upon a large wooden pail. I could not

see any of the crew, save the mate at my side; but from the constant tittering that proceeded from the rigging I could both locate them and understand that they were hugely enjoying the proceedings of the occasion. He now began to apply the lather to my face with a huge brush made of manilla rope. His bellowing never ceased for a moment. He covered my face and my head with the disgusting lather, and then, pulling his huge knife from his belt, he began to shave me with both his hands. This through with, I hoped the worst was over, and for a moment began to congratulate myself that I had finally passed the fiery ordeal. But Neptune did not propose to dismiss me without his benediction; so raising both hands and looking upward, as if for the blessing of the gods, he gave the wished-for signal, and instantly I was drenched, and almost drowned indeed, by a falling shower of sea-water. The crew had climbed to the yard-arm, under which I sat for my shaving, each armed with a bucket of water; and at the signal of Neptune they all dashed it upon me, amid loud bursts and roars of laughter from all sides. Old Neptune now told me that henceforth I could sail the seas without molestation from him.

The passengers had been aroused by the confusion and came on deck to witness the demonstration, but were prohibited from going forward until the ordeal was passed with me. The boy was now served in the same manner as I had been, when Mr. Watson had also to accept the attentions of Neptune. The invalid passenger, after numerous protestations, finally bought himself off with a dozen bottles of wine. To these the captain added another dozen, and the crew spent the night in a crazy carousal.

The next day they were not possessed of the happiest feelings. The mate was engaged in painting the bulwarks, when, on the approach of the steward, he began to find fault about the dinner. For some time words were exchanged in angry tone, when, finally, the mate picked up a handspike and struck the steward a fearful blow over the head. This blow felled the steward to the deck, and the mate, not yet satisfied, rushed upon him with his drawn knife, determined to end the life of his foe. The carpenter, who had once been mate, and had a special feeling against the present incumbent, now came to the rescue of the steward. The fight now became, for a few moments, general, until the captain, aroused to a sense of the situation, rushed on deck, and, revolver in hand, succeeded in quelling the disturbance and restoring order for the time. The men reluctantly dispersed to their several duties. During the day they kept up among themselves an undertone wrangling, and determined, before the day should pass, that they would throw the mate into the sea. The propitious time was watched for, and before night, on the captain going below, the steward attacked the mate, which was the signal for the entire crew to join in the fight against him. Several times they tried in vain to throw him over the bulwarks. They at last dealt him a severe blow, and were in the act of giving him to the sea, when the captain appeared on deck and threatened to shoot any and every one who attempted it. To my great surprise he again quelled the mutiny, and saved the life of the mate. Had they thrown the man overboard he must have perished, as the vessel was going at a high rate of speed. This was the last of the mutinous spirit, the balance of our voyage being tranquil in this respect.

We were now nearing our destination, and occasionally we would see a vessel. During the entire voyage, however, up to our nearing the port of Rio Janeiro, we had sighted but four vessels. Of these we spoke two, the sails of the others only being descried. Of the two we spoke, one was a foreign vessel and one was an American. This speaking a vessel is done, when near by, by means of the trumpet, a few general questions being asked and answered, concerning the vessel's name, destination, nativity, cargo, health, etc. When ships are more widely separated, signals are used in an ingenious way, by means of which all these general questions are covered. The sight of a ship at sea, where the voyage, like our own, is long, is exceedingly refreshing. All hands come on deck, and the moving sails are watched for hours with the utmost interest and anxiety. The depredations of the Alabama during this time made the appearance of American vessels much more of a rarity than usual. In ordinary times, on the voyage, we would have seen many vessels.

No opportunity offered for sending mail homeward, and as the letter written from Boston was not mailed by Mr. Clark, or, if so, never reached its destination, my parents were in perfect ignorance of my whereabouts since I parted with my father in Philadelphia. I would gladly have availed myself of a chance to inform them of my present surroundings; but no such opportunity was presented. Neither could I hear from home. Whether sick or well, dead or alive, I knew not. Of one thing I was certain, that with all my wickedness my mother's heart was still warm with love for her wayward son, and that daily her prayers would go up to God, who only knew where that son could be.

During the entire trip I saw no land myself, although the captain reported that several islands were sighted by his glass, and that once, when by head-winds we were driven much out of our way, he sighted as he thought the coast of Africa. But now we were nearing Rio Janeiro, and hugging the coast more closely each day. The towns along the coast were numerous, and some of them appeared very beautiful. Never before did the solid earth appear more lovely or more desirable to me. It was toward evening when we came near to the harbor of Rio Janeiro. We had seen the town miles away; and the beautiful Sugar-loaf Mountains served as a background of grandeur, lifting their heads in loveliness and beauty. Beacon-lights shone out from the lofty bluffs to illumine the path of the vessel toward the city and along the coast. Soon from the fort away we heard the signal-gun, which was accepted by the captain as a warning to drop anchor. And now a boat with the health-officer approached, and we received the gentleman on board. After an examination of the vessel and the condition of the crew was made we were permitted to move up the harbor and drop anchor before the city. The vessel was now thoroughly cleared, preparatory to discharging the cargo.

The morning after our arrival in the harbor,

Mr. Watson and the other passengers took boat for the shore. It seemed to me that I could not have them leave; that I belonged to and with these American passengers more than to this German ship and crew. The sorrow of my heart was most keen when they left, as I feared, forever, and in their boat disappeared from my view. Now I was alone, with not one friend on board! What should I do? By means of lighters we soon unloaded our ship. The passengers were gone, the ship's loading was ashore, and it seemed quite time for me to go too. Bum-boats daily visited our vessel with a great variety of luscious fruits for sale. These fruits looked tempting indeed; and though the crew bought freely of them, I had no money with which to buy, and must go without. In my anxiety to get away, I determined for a means of livelihood to leave the sea for ever. I had seen enough of it. My life, I also determined, should be reformed. Prodigal that I was, I would arise and go to my Father's house. And yet, would God receive a poor wretch like me? Would he give me a place under the shadow and shelter of his gracious wings? Wicked as I knew myself to be, yet I doubted not that the Father's love covered even *my* miserable case.

Seventy-six days I had been on the sea. I had been shipped at $25 per month; but of the total

amount of my wages Mr. Clark had taken $50,
leaving me something short of $15 as my rightful
due.   Yet this small amount I greatly needed ; and
I said to the mate that I wished to settle and be
put on shore.   He said the captain was busy, and
I should wait until to-morrow.   Accordingly, I
waited until the morrow came, when I approached
the captain and asked to be paid off, that I might
go ashore.   He swore he would hang me on the
fore-yard of his ship before he would pay me anything whatever.   I dared not approach him again,
but begged piteously to be put ashore.   Days rolled on, and meantime the captain and the crew were
frequently on shore.   Evidently I was not to be
allowed to go ashore, but was to be compelled to
sail with them again.   I began to enter the dark
valley of despair.   There seemed to be no daylight and no deliverance for me.   What should I
do?   Had I no friend in man; and had God himself at last forsaken me?   Would he not provide
for my deliverance, and plan a way for my escape?
I saw nowhere the signs of the rising star of day.
Had God indeed cast me off forever?   Had he
quite forgotten to be gracious?   Perhaps he would
yet providentially deliver me.

One afternoon I heard the splash of oars, and
going to the vessel's side, lo, and behold, my
old friend Watson was climbing the ladder from a

boat to the ship's deck. He grasped me kindly by
the hand, and asked after my health. I now felt
that my last chance had come, and that I must
speedily and faithfully improve it. Mr. Watson
had come aboard unexpectedly to both himself
and the crew. When he left he never thought to
return again; but, providentially for me, he had
forgotten something of his effects, and for this he
returned. I called him aside, and gave a brief account of the treatment I had received from the
captain in his absence. He stood a moment in
thoughtful silence, and then said, "Come with me."
I thought I saw relief, if not release, in the gentleman's eye and motion, and with boldness and
alacrity I followed him. He led the way to the
captain, and at once and quite emphatically inquired why he had not settled with me, and why
he had not allowed me to go ashore. The captain
manifested indignation at the seeming interference
of Mr. Watson, and angrily replied. They both
descended into the cabin for further talk. On their
return to deck the captain's boat was lowered, and
Mr. Watson's forgotten goods were placed in it.
Mr. Watson now told me to descend to the boat.
How my heart bounded with joy and gratitude.
When aboard the boat, Mr. Watson reminded me
that I had not my clothing. Indeed, I had not
thought of it, and cared but little for it at

the thought of being free. He directed me to return for them. The captain objected to my taking them, but Mr. Watson insisted and prevailed. I was soon in the boat again with my deliverer, and this time with my personal effects. The boat in an instant was more of home to me than ever the ship had been. A row of fifteen minutes brought us to the wharf, and I was allowed once more to step on God's solid earth.

CHAPTER XXVIII.

FRIENDS IN A STRANGE LAND.

For three months I had paced the deck, with only the rolling seas beneath me; now I was on land again, though thousands of miles from my own native clime. In the whole continent of South America I knew but three human beings besides the crew of the vessel I had left; and of these I should see again only Mr. Watson. On getting on the wharf I found men busily engaged in unloading boats, and in other wharf-labor, talking in a most excited though natural manner, in a language I had never before heard. It was Spanish, and to me in very pleasant contrast with the German. The tone was very excited, and yet I soon learned that in the coolest moments this was customary.

Mr. Watson left me in the office of a ship-chandler and went out for a short time to attend to some business, promising, however, to return for me soon. According to his promise, he returned. Meantime I enjoyed my stay. I was in an American store, the merchants being American and their language the English. Never before did my language sound so dear to me. Mr. Watson congratulated me in getting out of Sourbier's hands, and told me to see to it that I kept myself out of them. The captain had insisted that I should return again, and thus had objected to my taking my clothing. What the promise of Mr. Watson was, I do not know; but what his personal determination and advice were, I was now made to understand. He proposed to take me to the consul's office, and see what could be done for me. We stepped into a carriage drawn by two mules, driven by a Spaniard, and after a brief ride through narrow streets were halted at the American consul's office. Mr. Watson at once acquainted the consul with the general circumstances of my case, speaking largely and with excited interest and sympathy from his own experience. The consul, whose name memory fails to serve me, manifested much indignation over the recital, and kindly told me to feel easy, assuring me that he would do all in his power for me. He wrote me a permit to the hospital, and assured me that I should want for nothing; also, that I should be sent to my northern and native home as soon as possible. How wonderful this talk and these expressions of sympathy and humanity seemed to me. In a moment the dark clouds that had been gathering for months were silver-lined, or gone. If ever gratitude well-

ed up in my bosom it was then, and in that spot.
I began to feel that God had not forgotten me, and
that he was raising up friends that would show
me needed mercy.

Mr. Watson now had our carriage driven through
the city for half an hour or so, to a fine large building known as the hospital, to the accommodations
and immunities of which my permit from the consul gave me the liberty.   I was led into the office
of the house, where my name was taken, together
with those of my parents, my residence, etc.; and
many questions were asked me bearing on my own
life and late history.   The name of my vessel—the
Vincie—was also taken.   This institution I found
to be under the management of the Catholics, like
Brazil, in its general interests.   A bell was rung,
and a sister of charity, a large Spanish woman,
appeared and took me in charge.   Here I bid Mr.
Watson good-by, he promising to call and see me
soon again.   I was conducted to the bath-room,
where, after washing, I was furnished with a linen
suit throughout, even including hat and slippers.
I was now led to the hair-dresser, where I was
closely trimmed, and then conducted to the sitting-
room of the establishment.   Here were a dozen
young men, among whom were several Americans,
and one Philadelphian with the rest.   The reader
may well imagine that this wonderful change from

the condition and life of the ship was an appreciated relief, and that the company into which I had fallen was an agreeable surprise to me.

From the hour of my entrance to the hospital I received from the sisters the kindest possible treatment, and many little tokens of genuine Christian love. Two of them spoke English quite fluently, and this, with my American companions, made me feel from the first quite at home. The English, as a language, never seemed to me more beautiful and charming than now.

During my three months' stay Mr. Watson often called and showed me very many acts of kindness, thereby endearing himself for all time to my heart. He was seeking constantly to find for me a passage homeward; and one day he brought with him the captain of a vessel bound for California, by way of Cape Horn. It was not known, from the depredations of the Alabama, that any other way would soon offer. This captain kindly volunteered to take me through to San Francisco without charge, and thought that from there I could easily get home to my father. The captain of the California vessel was not yet ready to embark, entertaining fears of the Alabama, perhaps, which had lately been in the port of Rio Janeiro. Before the time for his sailing Captain Plummer arrived at the port, intending soon to sail for New York;

and Mr. Watson kindly arranged with him for my homeward passage. Captain Plummer personally assured me that he would gladly take me, and see that I had every kindness. He was to sail in a single week.

The sisters came to me privately and almost protested against my going from them. They said I was in poor health, and needed the best of attention, and that if I would I could permanently remain in their hospital and hospitable home. Indeed, the temptation was strong; but I knew that with all their kindness there were open arms and warm hearts awaiting my coming in the dear old home of my childhood. They sought to magnify the dangers of the deep, and brought freshly to my mind the sufferings I had endured. As a final argument, they said a distinguished Parisian doctor was to arrive in a few weeks, and his advice and treatment would be valuable to me. I ought at least to stay and see him. However, I determined to go home with Captain Plummer, and all necessary arrangements were made for the voyage.

Just before the day of sailing, however, Mr. Watson called again, bringing with him Captain Thomson, bound for Baltimore. He was to sail in one month; and if I would tarry for him an opportunity would offer for an interview with the French physician. A sick lady was also desirous of my place on Captain Plummer's ship, and I was asked to give way to her. Of course I consented, and yet felt exceedingly dejected at the prospect of tarrying in Brazil a full month. The doctor came, as was expected, and a careful examination of my eyes followed. At the close of the inspection he remarked to one of the sisters, "*No sta-bone*," which I was afterward informed meant "no good," or "no use." He then told me that I could have no help; that finally my eyes would go speedily, but might possibly last me a full year. Thus his voice but confirmed the dread decree against me of the Philadelphia physicians; and I began to realize more fully now than ever that I must become blind at last. The conclusion was horrible to me, and served to increase the longing of my heart to get to my own father's home again. But I must patiently wait now for the set time of Captain Thomson. The way was provided, and soon I should be homeward bound.

During my stay in Brazil no opportunity had offered for me to send mail north, and no word had I been able to communicate to my home. Little did I know of the anxiety and the misery of those dear home hearts. Meantime I was resting comfortably as a stranger in one of the most interesting countries of the world. I knew Brazil to be the leading nation of the South American continent, and really the second nation in importance, extent, and population of the new world

A few words of this nation and country here may not be out of place, and in keeping with the plan of this autobiography. The territorial area of South America is 6,959,000 square miles, while Brazil has an area of 3,252,900 square miles, or nearly one half of all. The population of the continent is 25,675,000, and that of Brazil is 10,000,000, or about two fifths of all. It is the only monarchy within South America, and in an independent sense the only one in the new world. Brazil was discovered May 3d, 1500, by Vincente Yanes Pincon, a companion of Columbus, and was soon after taken possession of by Pedro Alvarez Cabral. Brazil continued as a province of Portugal until 1822, when Dom Pedro I., father of the present sovereign, declared Brazil free and independent of the home government. April 7th, 1831, Dom Pedro abdicated in favor of his son, a child of but five years of age. A regency of three persons conducted the government until 1840, when Dom Pedro was declared of age, though only in his fifteenth year. On July 18th, 1841, he was crowned as emperor. In 1866 the emperor emancipated his own slaves, and in 1871 the legislature provided for the gradual emancipation of the slaves of the entire empire.

The religion of the state is Roman Catholic; but since 1811 other religions have been tolerated. The Protestant population is probably short of 50,000; but great progress is being made by the missionaries of the various Protestant bodies. From present indications, the disestablishment of the Roman Catholic Church will be realized at no distant day. The people have very small confidence in the priesthood, and their influence is waning in proportion as civilization and education advance. The press has a large degree of liberty, and is severely outspoken against the intolerance and corruption of the Roman Church. The policy of the present emperor is exceedingly enlightened, and he is everywhere encouraging the establishment of good and free schools. Dom Pedro is at this time (June, 1876,) traveling in the United States, and is everywhere welcomed and honored as a worthy representative of the throne.

Brazil is much more prolific in both animal and vegetable forms of life than any other part of the known world. The butterflies, for example, are most beautiful and numerous. All the known species of Europe number but 390, while those observed in the town of Para, Brazil, alone number 700 distinct species. Prof. Agassiz found in the Amazon alone 1,163 new species of fish, which is more than the entire Mediterranean Sea produces.

13

Rio Janeiro, or, as more commonly known, Rio, is possessed of the finest harbor not only in South America, but all over the known world. It is also regarded as the safest; and it is certainly the most capacious. Its entrance is marked by a remarkable hill resembling in form a sugar-loaf—whence its name. This attains the hight of 900 feet, and is from the sea a most conspicuous and beautiful presentation. This is on the west side of the bay or harbor, while on the opposite side, at a distance of one and one half miles, stands the fort of Santa Cruz, on which is a light-house. On the bosom, and beautifully bestudding the bay, lie something like 100 islands, some in a high state of cultivation. The dock-yard and marine establishments are found on one of these harbor islands. There being no obstructions, ships may enter the harbor day or night, while the navies of the world, and indeed their entire shipping, may ride comfortably upon its capacious bosom.   .

The city is surrounded by an amphitheater of hills and mountains, which present a beautiful spectacle from the bay. The population is about 400,000, making it not only the most important commercial city of South America, but also the most populous. As the capital of the country, it contains the palace of the emperor, and other state buildings, together with a beautiful cathedral on a

lofty eminence commanding the sea; also several
convents, hospitals, and other institutions of charity. The general architecture of the city is not
prepossessing; but the streets are well laid out,
intersecting each other at right angles, while they
are paved with heavy blocks of granite, and have
central water-courses. The moral habits of the
people are not what one would wish, and do not
speak very well for the controlling church. Sunday is observed chiefly as a gala day; and in the
sense that Protestants of America respect and observe it, it is not known.

One beautiful morning, as I was enjoying the
breeze and a delicious orange, suddenly my friend
Mr. Watson came upon me and said, hurriedly, "My boy, I have come for you. The vessel is ready to sail, and now you can go home."
In the excitement of the moment my feelings quite
overcame me. Was it indeed true that I might
embark for my own home! Though in almost
daily expectation of the announcement, yet I was
surprised when it came. The place, too, had come
to seem like home to me. Everything had been
so pleasant, and all had been so kind, that but for
the loved ones at home I could willingly have remained forever.

The sisters, when it was known that I must go,
remembered me with many presents; and this gave

me new assurances of their kindness and love. Tearfully I bid them good-by, and received their parting blessings.

With Mr. Watson as a guide, after a brisk walk of half an hour we were again at the ship-chandler's office, where I had first came on landing. I was kindly entertained, and much conversation ensued touching my treatment on board Captain Sourbier's German ship. I was shown a chest containing my own clothing, all neatly washed and ironed, and two other entire suits. This, I was told, was all my own. I felt proud, rich, and grateful, as may well be imagined by the reader. I was now taken on board the ship, Mr. Watson accompanying me, and seeing me safely in the hands of Captain Thomson. He now bid me a fatherly good-by, and at parting said, "May God bless you, my boy." My heart was too full to do more than say good-by.

I parted from the man who had shown me most marvelous kindness. Never more should I look upon his face in life. The man who had proved himself the sent of God to me was gradually receding from my vision. I trust God heard, recorded, and answered the prayers with which I followed his receding form. Never did a child of Adam more deeply need a friend than I, in my forsaken, lonely, wretched, and almost dying condition; and never did a truer, nobler, and more deserving friend appear in behalf of a suffering fellow than Mr. Watson, the merchant stranger of New York. If Heaven remembers and rewards a cup of cold water given to a suffering disciple, what will not Heaven do for a man whose acts of Christian devotion and disinterested love had, even toward this humble child, been numbered by hundreds and thousands? How much he did for me, I shall never know; how much I loved and reverenced the man for his devotion, he can never know. I hope to meet him in heaven, and from a grateful heart, a heart that then can see all things in their true light, thank him once more. Until then, my prayers shall arise to Him that sitteth upon the throne for a daily blessing on his head and his home.

That I now retrospected my life with bitter tears, no one can doubt; and that I formed good resolutions for the future, none can wonder. After experiencing all that I had, it would be both ungenerous and inhuman not to be grateful to God, who had never for one moment forsaken me. I vowed before my Master that I would reform my life and yield him my heart in willing and devoted service. He should have practical demonstrations of my sincerity and of my gratitude. I craved anew his protecting care for my journey over the deep,

angry sea, and pleaded with him to lead me in safety to my father's door and my mother's arms. I
would humble myself like the prodigal at their
feet; I would give them tokens of my repentance,
and prove the fervency of my love and devotion.
I knew that as God had, so would my parents accept and receive and forgive me.

CHAPTER XXIX.

THE HOMEWARD VOYAGE.

The crew were taking aboard the balance of their cargo, consisting chiefly of coffee. All seemed happy and contented in their labor; and with the creaking of the tackle was heard the merry shout and the good-natured rally of the men. They were with one or two exceptions Americans, and the language of all was my own mother-tongue. Our vessel was a full-rigged bark, —the Agnes,—belonging to Baltimore, commanded by Captain Thomson, and manned by a crew of some fifteen men. The ship was new and stout, and in general appearance and arrangements much like a home of comfort. Its route was from Baltimore to Rio Janeiro, and it was built expressly for the coffee trade. Captain Thomson was a tall, well-proportioned man, of some sixty years. He was hearty and healthy, but gray of beard. He was full of kindness and genial cordiality. He received me on board with much kindness, and tenderly inquired after my health, expressing hope for its improvement. At his instance I gave him a detailed account of my former experience with Captain Sourbier, at which he expressed much indignation, and assured me that from him I could depend on attention and sympathy. Indeed, the general appearance of the captain, crew, and ship inspired me at sight with a feeling of content and satisfaction. The dinner provided was most relishable, and consisted of every delicacy and comfort that one could wish. It was in wonderful contrast with that furnished by the German ship. Instead of being placed back in a gloomy bunk of the forecastle, I was provided with a pleasant state-room for my own exclusive use, neatly and comfortably furnished. My meals were sometimes brought to my room; but usually I sat at the captain's table, and fared as he fared in everything.

In the course of the afternoon my chest was brought to my room, and the keys thereof given into my hands. Of course, I promptly made a general survey of the contents, a survey which, though prompted somewhat by curiosity, served to awaken new and fervent gratitude toward my dear old benefactor, Mr. Watson. Besides two complete suits of clothing,—the one for warm and tropical weather and the other for cold and northern weather,—I found an abundance of underclothing and outer garments adapted to my wants in every way. No want was forgotten or unsupplied. A mother, from a rich treasury and from a heart of richer affection, could have done little more than this God-given friend and Christian benefactor had done for me. Had I been his own child I could have said, "Father, you have done enough, and deserve my fullest love." Neither had he forgotten the appetite, but from that rich, tropical climate had selected of its choicest delicacies in the line of fruits, etc., and placed them carefully in my chest. Could a mother have been more thoughtful, or a father more considerate? Was it not enough that he had secured my passage free and a place for me at the captain's own table? It was enough to awaken everlasting gratitude; but not all, as the reader shall yet be made to understand.

After a refreshing sleep, preceded, I am sure, by grateful prayers and a trustful resigning of my life to the Father's care, I was early awakened by the merry singing of the crew. I was on deck in season to witness the hoisting of the anchor, the loosening of the sails, and the general preparation for getting under way, and on the homeward voyage. Among the sailors there was no wrangling and no confusion; few loud words were heard, and nothing that bore the faintest resemblance to an oath. Indeed, during the entire voyage of several months I did not hear a single oath from any of the crew. I do not know that there was the least inclination to profanity. The rules of Captain Thomson would admit of no oath aboard his ship. As I sat down to breakfast our goodly ship began to move out under the gentle breeze, and at last I was homeward bound. The breeze that fanned the sea and the gale which swept the ocean should bear me home. God directed both, and under his protecting hand should I sail.

What a merciful Providence had overshadowed me, and how wonderful the change he had wrought in my behalf. Three months before I was lying on shipboard in this harbor with no friend on board, and knowing not that I had one single friend within my reach. I felt that God had quite cast me off, and had forgotten me in his anger forever. Insults, threats, and death itself, stared me blankly in the face, and I knew not which way nor where to turn for the simplest help or smallest comfort. No one in all the world could reach me with one word of love or one smile of sympathy. But now might I say, "What hath God wrought, and why is his providence so gracious toward me?" Every benefit I possessed I owed, and now, bless his name, I owned, to him. Had I friends, comforts, luxuries indeed; they were all from that Father's hand from whom cometh every good and perfect gift, and who looks down with favor upon the falling sparrow and crying raven, and even numbereth the hairs of our weary heads. Well might I trust in him, and suffer his guidance of my feet in the way.

Now we were sailing out of the harbor into the bay; and the city which had afforded me protection and given me a home and the tokens of tender love was receding from my gaze. Surely never more should I see it in its loveliness and grandeur, until from on high I should look down upon it; and then, could I hold the cup, surely I would pour forth blessings with grateful remembrance upon the people. All day long we were sailing down the bay, hovering close to the land, as if dreading to release our hold upon its protecting wings. Even when the shades of evening crept over us the coast and the crowning hills thereof were near; and until my own retirement for the night the lights of the homes upon the not distant shore sent forth their dim and twinkling rays as if to lighten our way on the deep. Nature had veiled her face in the cloud of darkness, but the Lord of nature still gave us tokens of his friendly presence. In the morning, as I arose, I looked shoreward, instinctively hoping for one more sight of the friendly coast of Brazil; but all was in vain, for distance had sunken the land in the sea and dissolved the forms of the towering peaks, and the face of the deep only was visible to my gaze. I was out upon the raging billows again, and yet sailing, I felt, as in the hollow of the Master's hand.

Captain Plummer, with whom I had intended sailing, was delayed longer than he expected, and his vessel set sail only the day before the one on which we sailed. The captain of our ship was continually on the lookout for him; and ten days or so after sailing we sighted his vessel, but were not near enough to speak her. The time dragged on quite heavily and wearily from having no labor and from inability to read. This was a wonderful privation to me, as I had spent much time over literature, and felt therefore the more need of it. The lessons of the page, however, were now too dim; they had faded forever from my sight. It cheered me, nevertheless, to know that the face of man was yet distinct, and that with the daylight I could get about without help. The dimness of my vision was gradually increasing, and yet I trusted that sight would not altogether go until I could once more see the faces of father, mother, sisters, and brother. It would not be enough, I thought, to clasp their hands and hear their words; I must see them too.

Though unable to read myself, yet I was highly

favored in this line. On board our ship was a boy
of some fifteen years, a nephew of the captain.
He afforded me much company, and showed me
great kindness withal. He was a Catholic boy (and
I also supposed the captain to be a Catholic), but was
evidently much devoted to the Master's will. One
day soon after sailing he came to my room and
offered, at the suggestion of the captain, to read for
me. He also proposed to read from the Bible, which
he largely did. The readings included many of my
old Sabbath-school lessons, and were both interesting and refreshing to me. Never did God's
word seem more sublime and more worthy the lips
of Him who spake as never man spake.

The time wore on pleasantly, and great kindness
was shown me by all. Perfect harmony, too, prevailed among the men, and the evenings were
usually spent in inspiring song. A Mr. Richards,
an Englishman, was a fine vocalist, while several
others of the crew understood the use of various
instruments. These were in frequent use, and,
with the songs, were truly inspiring. "We are
out on the ocean sailing," was a frequent song, and
much enjoyed by all. No labor was performed on
the Sabbath, except such as the sailing of the ship
absolutely required. This was in great contrast
with what transpired on Captain Sourbier's ship
and in the capital Catholic city of Rio Janeiro.

For the crew of the one and the inhabitants of the other, in the usual American acceptation, there was no Sabbath.

After sailing several weeks with an almost constantly pleasant sea, I learned from the captain that it was his purpose to put into St. Thomas, that he might register his vessel as a means of security against the Alabama and other rebel craft. A few days after this information we were cheered with the announcement from the man at the foretop, "Land ho." This cry on shipboard is often electrifying, and under the circumstances was particularly so to us. After we had nearly approached St. Thomas we discovered a sail, which, to the joy of all, proved to be that of the vessel of Captain Plummer. He was also putting into St. Thomas for the same purpose. The wind became boisterous toward night, and our captain determined to lay aback until the morning before risking the entrance to the harbor. Captain Plummer, however, was more resolute, and he passed on, entering the channel and the harbor safely that night. The next morning after dropping anchor in the harbor Captain Plummer came on board, with whom we had a pleasant visit. From him, however, I learned the dreadful news that the sick lady to whom I had given up my room had died when they were two weeks out from Rio Janeiro. This intelligence

pletely unnerved me, for from my own feelings
ıew how intensely anxious she must have been
each the loved ones at home. Of course, they
e obliged also to bury her at sea.

> "Not in the church-yard should she sleep,
>   Amid its silent gloom;
> She died upon the mighty deep,
>   And there she found her tomb.

> "For her broke not the grassy turf,
>   Nor turned the dewy sod;
> Her dust shall rest beneath the surf,
>   Her spirit with her God."

ev. Dr. Cuyler speaks as follows of a burial at
as witnessed by himself. The body was that
ı man; and the man was a miserable, drunken
ture, whose death few mourned, save in sym-
ıy for the weeping wife and dependent children:
After the summary fashion on shipboard, the
y was inclosed in blankets, bound around with
ɜ of rope, and stretched upon a plank. To the
a large weight was attached, and the whole
then swung over the ship's side and made
with ropes. Soon the boatswain piped all
ls to burial. When the poor widow had come
ʳard and taken her seat on a little cabin-stool
ʾor the purpose, with her two children by her
, the captain commenced reading the burial
ice. When the captain had concluded the

words, 'We therefore commit his body to the deep,' the signal was given, a heavy splash was heard, and the body sunk like lead in the mighty waters. A few bubbles rose to the surface, which were the only memorials that shall ever rise to mark his resting-place."

Of more than six months spent on the sea, I had witnessed no death, and was spared the deep solemnities of a sea-burial.

Our vessel lay in the harbor some ten days while registering, but feeling badly I chose not to go ashore or into the town. The bum-boats came thickly about us, as in the harbor of Rio Janeiro; and though this time I had no money at personal command, yet the captain kindly anticipated every wish and supplied every want. We took in a supply of fresh water, paying therefor four cents a gallon. There happens to be no water on the island, save what is caught in cisterns; and while this supply is poor, it is also often quite short. St. Thomas is a small island of but thirty-seven square miles and 8,000 inhabitants. It belongs to Denmark, with Santa Cruz and St. John, two small contiguous islands of the West India group. Their total area is but 190 square miles, and their total population 46,000. When we emerged from the Danish harbor of St. Thomas we flung the flag of a foreign nation to the breeze; and we sailed hence-ι with a feeling of security, so far as rebel craft concerned.

ᵀe now began to realize that we were approach- a northern clime, and that much differ- ι existed between January in the tropics and uary in the North.   The thicker suit was made ·eplace the thinner one, and again I was re- ded of my providential friend.   A few days and we spake a trader from New York, ob- ing some fresh provision and some American ɜrs.   The weather now, besides being cold, also specially threatening, and even more so ι I realized.   The captain was manifestly anx- .   He called me to him while on deck, and asked into the cabin for a little talk.   He said the ipects were too favorable for a furious storm, as it was possible that we might be cast away vished to make some further information of a matter of record.   Also, he had something ell me of my friend Mr. Watson, which, for of possible contingencies, he would defer no ɟer.   He then produced a package containing ɼell-filled money-belt, saying, "Mr. Watson ιed me to hand this to you at the end of the ιge."   He placed it in my hands, and I found ιite heavy.   At the same time he offered to ɔ charge of it if I desired.   Although anxious ιake an examination of it, I desired him to do

14

so, and returned it to his hand. I was filled with surprise at this new and wholly unexpected manifestation from Mr. Watson, and most deeply regretted that I had no knowledge of his address, or even of his first name. To Mr. Thomson, as well as to myself, Mr. Watson was a complete stranger. Surely God had cared for me in the midst of my want and my wickedness.

We now had a long siege of heavy weather. The wind was north-west, and it bore us rain, snow, and sleet, and everything soon became a sheet of ice. Our barometer became deranged, and the compass would not work. Of course, we lost our reckoning, and for several days, in the midst of this trying storm, we knew not where we were. After the subsidence of the wind a dense fog and a heavy sea succeeded, amid which no man could live on deck. The man at the wheel was lashed to his place, and the crew took refuge in the rigging. The captain was both anxious and nervous, and scarcely eat anything while the storm prevailed. At last, however, in the good providence of God the sky cleared, the storm ceased, and the sea became tranquil again. A few days of pleasant sailing, and the joyful news rang out once more that land was within sight.

At Cape Henry we were boarded by a pilot, who took charge of our vessel in its passage up the

Chesapeake. And now I was in familiar waters again. I naturally recalled my experience on the old oyster-craft, and felt somewhat at home in waters which I had plowed before. On account of a dense fog on arriving at the mouth of the Patapsco River, we cast anchor for the night. During the night the density of the fog greatly increased, so that the pilot observed that from the dimness of our lights we could not easily be discerned. About midnight all hands were aroused, and the pilot informed us that our vessel was in the exact line of a large iron steamer that plied between Norfolk and Baltimore; that it was about due, and that from the dense fog we were really in great danger. We must either remove from its line, in which we did not succeed, or apprise the steamer in some way of our whereabouts. A half hour or so elapsed, when we heard the whistle of the advancing steamer, and soon the not-distant sound of her paddle-wheels. Extra lights had been placed in the masts, and the men were hallooing themselves hoarse; but evidently, from the direction of the steamer, we were not observed. Finally some combustible matter was set on fire on the deck, the flame of which caught the eye of the wheelsman on the steamer, who by a special effort barely cleared us. The alarm aboard was very great, for had she struck us we could not have been saved. It really looked as though we were to perish at the very doors of our homes.

All went well next day until we were within some twelve miles of Baltimore, when we were stopped once more by floating ice. We could now neither advance nor recede. While lying here a propeller, loaded with powder and having on board a number of army officers, undertook to go up the narrow channel just opened by the ice-boat. The Norfolk steamer, however, was coming down, and in attempting to pass the propeller was bulged, and her stoves upset. The crew and passengers were taken off by the steamer, which passed on by us down the river. But the propeller was now ablaze, and in this condition floated past us, and in a few moments sunk. Luckily the powder had not been reached before sinking; and, for our further comfort at the time, we did not apprehend that her cargo was powder.

The third day the ice cleared, and we were taken by the tug-boat to the city. The captain and other officers went to their homes, but I remained aboard until the morning. They were greeted by their loved ones, and I was near to my own deserted home; but whether all or any of my kin remained, I knew not. Were the dear parents still alive, or had they in sorrow gone down to the grave? I should soon know; and perhaps the revelation of death would stand against me in my own home. How much of sunshine I had received within that home, of such real comfort, of such solid bliss. Whether death had crossed its threshold or not, I had sent many shadows athwart it, and had filled with gloom its every room. Deep-drawn sighs had escaped a father's breast, and a mother's heart had been but little more than a tomb of grief. I had buried myself, while yet alive, as one dead within her heart. And yet I knew, without one passing doubt, that if alive that mother could and would forgive, and if dead she would watch and guide me with an angel's love. How I longed ere I slept to lift the curtain that concealed my home. With a fervent prayer for each and all of them I sunk into the unconsciousness of sleep, for the last time on shipboard.

The morning came at last, and therewith the captain, according to nis word. He at once handed me the money-belt, which he had never opened, and I counted out seventy dollars in gold, besides some silver pieces for pocket use. The captain gave me a new belt, and securing my money in this I placed it for safety around my body. Whether this money came from Mr. Watson's own hands, as I have reason to believe it did, probably I shall never know. It could not have come from Sourbier, as he only owed me at most some fteen

dollars.   To Mr. Watson I give the credit, whatever its source; and while I live I shall bless his
name as that of a most gracious and wonderful
benefactor.   The captain had brought his carriage
with him, and in this I rode with him to the depot.
He purchased me a ticket for Philadelphia, bought
me a lunch, and saw me aboard the train.   Nor
did he forget the cordial good-by and the generous
blessing.   Captain Thomson had well done his
part, and next to Mr. Watson I felt that he was
my greatest benefactor.   I think he gave me a free
passage on his vessel, and provided for me while
thereon from his own bounty gratuitously.   This
was certainly very much, and yet all was exceeded
by his extreme kindness and fatherly care.   While
life lasts the memory of Captain Thomson, of Baltimore, will be fresh in my heart; and from my
heart I shall beseech the good Father to reward
him well.

CHAPTER XXX.

HOME AGAIN.

I had now escaped the sea and its dangers; and, flying on the swifter wings of steam, I felt a wonderful security. We were detained at Havre de Grace ferry several hours, however, by the ice blockade, and did not reach Philadelphia until midnight. With difficulty I arranged for transference to the Episcopal Hospital, four miles away, but finally made the necessary arrangement, and was soon again at the old refuge where years before I had found shelter and protection with kindness and love. The same old nurse received me; and although it was long before day, yet the superintendent, Mr. Knight, from whom many kindnesses had come in my former stay, was called up. He greeted me kindly, but showed great surprise. I counted my money into his hands for safe keeping; and after a bath I retired for rest.

The next day many old friends yet in the hospital called at my room and greeted me with great kindness. I was grateful for these demonstrations of friendship, and yet felt that there was an aching void which friends not of my own blood could not fill. I wanted to hear from home. It was but an hour's ride by steam to my old home, now at Doylestown, and my heart yearned to know that it was well with them. Mr. Knight called early in the forenoon, and to him I related my story as it was. He expressed much astonishment, but kindly volunteered to write to my father at once Returning in a few moments to my bed-side,—for I was unable to arise, from the excitement of the occasion,—he wrote as follows:

"MR. SMITH:

"*Dear Sir*—Your son Andrew is again with us. He is suffering with the old trouble. Will you come immediately?"

My reflections during the day were of a most serious nature. I wondered if my folks were indeed alive, and full of the old, deep love for me. And could they receive me again as their own son to their home and their hearts? This was even more than I had a right to ask; but I knew full well, from the great depth of their love, that I might with confidence expect all of this. I had left a home of sunshine and comfort, and wandered forth in quest of honor and happiness, which fictitious writings had painted as the ideal of my fancy, and as a possible realization. Not for a

thousand worlds would I trace the way again. I
had gone by a rugged road, had suffered much,
and yet had by a loving God been safely led.
Surely the life saved by God belonged to him, and
to him I felt determined it should be given.

The day was spent as pleasantly as my own anxiety and the general circumstances would admit.
The physicians of the establishment, Dr. Morris
and his colleague, made a careful examination of
my eyes, and after consultation gave me their can-
did and generous advice. In view of the fact that
the disease of my eyes would ultimately destroy
them, they thought it best that I begin to prepare
myself for this event by learning the lessons which
one who is blind would need to understand for his
own happiness and efficiency. With the little
sight I had, I could greatly aid myself in these ac-
quisitions, and, by the system of instruction I
would follow, measurably prepare myself for an
event which could not at best be greatly delayed.
From their connection with the Pennsylvania Institution for the Instruction of the Blind, they
would do what they could, if I would consent, to secure me admission therein. Not only would they apply for me, but they would see that the necessary papers were made out, and would also write my parents
a letter of explanation and counsel. This was exceedingly kind of them, and I am sure I felt very grateful

for the interest taken and the kindness expressed
by the noble gentlemen. Had I made application
for admittance, and followed the usual course, I
might have waited months before I could have
gained admission. The institution could accommodate only a limited number, and was then full.
In 1875 there were within the state fifty-one persons who had made formal application for admission, and were waiting for their regular turns. At
the time of my entrance many were impatiently
waiting. During the day, several ladies of the
hospital who ministered in spiritual as well as
material ways called at my room and read to me
from the Word, and offered fervent prayers in my
behalf. These prayers, while they consoled, also
lifted largely the veil from my own heart, and painfully exposed to my view my many deep and
angry sins. Their sympathetic appeals for my
anxious mother, and their mention of her deep,
undying love for her dependent and wayward boy,
were well calculated to touch the heart of the
prodigal son that I was.

The day passed away, and therewith came no
tidings from home. The shadows of the evening
gathered about my bed again, and amid my anxious wonderings regarding home and home friends
I fell into a deep and refreshing sleep. With the
return of day I felt much better, and was able to

eat heartily and to dress. While reclining upon
my bed about 9:00 A. M. I heard quick footsteps
in the hall, and turning my eyes I saw Mr. Knight
and my own father approaching my bed. Nearly
two years had passed since I had seen my father's
face for the last time at the street-corner in Philadelphia; but now the same dear man was before
me again. He approached my bed, grasped my
hand, and, convulsed with emotion, cried, "My boy,
my boy." Nothing more could he say, and nothing whatever did I say. He held my hand; and
I could but hang my head, with a heart breaking
with sorrow. I could think of little more than
my guilt; and this seemed like a mountain that
forbade my approach to my father. This, thought
I, must first of all be removed; and how to compass
this end I hardly knew. My soul prompted me
to confess my great sin and plead his forgiveness;
but I did not yield to this better persuasion. I
asked Mr. Knight for my belt, and I poured my
gold into my father's hands. I felt somehow that
this might be accepted by him as an atoning offering. This action seemed to break the spell of
silence, and we entered into a brief conversation,
covering my wanderings and my final arrival in
Philadelphia. I wanted to inquire of my mother,
sisters, and brother, but feared to do so, lest my
father might say of one or all that they were dead.

To my relief, Mr. Knight inquired after the health of the family, when my father said, "All but Willie are well; he is poorly." This gave me wonderful relief. My dear mother, then, was alive, and death had not crossed the threshold of my father's home during my absence. How, in silence, I thanked God for these glad and blessed tidings; for though I could cruelly leave them, yet in my heart I loved them fervently, and would have died for the defense of either.

My father had brought a carriage to the door, and, preceded by my chest, I descended to it. I was made comfortable, and soon we were on our drive for the depot. I naturally expected that with every word my father would mention my conduct, and speak words of justly-deserved reproof. In the thought and expectation of this I was inclined to say very little. But no word of reproof came from him. Every act was an act of love looking to my comfort, and every word was the embodiment of real affection. No correction and no reproof made me feel a deeper sense of guilt. I saw the deep goodness of the man against whom I had so grossly sinned.

Once at the depot, a brief time was spent in waiting for the train; and several old friends advanced and spoke with us. To all of these my father, with deep emotion and choked utterance, said,

"My boy has come back; I have found my son." Of course my singular disappearance and long continued absence was a matter of knowledge to a great many, and on all hands old friends had sympathized with the sorrows of my parents. Though they knew not where I was, yet they had not given me up, and hoped and looked continually for my return. The letter from Mr. Knight had but answered the daily hope and confident expectation of their hearts. "He will come back again," was the ever-recurring protest, and the constant conviction of my mother.

The train in readiness, we were soon seated and ready for our departure to Doylestown. An hour's ride, and I stood once more on the old depot platform, and within forty rods of the beating, anxious heart of my own dear mother. Dear Willie was at the depot, and the first to meet me with his warm, sweet kiss. The dear boy looked quite pale and feeble; and it seemed as though his hold on this life was by a slender and brittle thread. Ten summers had passed over him on earth, and he had greatly changed since I saw him last. We walked in almost unbroken silence across the field to our home. I cared not to say much, and my father was inclined not to talk. I was wondering how I could meet my dear, dear mother; how I could ever again look into that face of love. I felt

that it would smite me for my guilt by telling me
of a heart which I had broken by my own cruel
sins. As we walked in silence, I painfully glanced
toward my father, whose long white locks now
seemed grayer than ever. His head was bowed,
and it seemed to me that with his every step he
was engaged in prayer for me, his wayward son,
and for the wife and mother whose heart was aching for my coming. As we walked side by side I
felt that we presented a true *tableau* of real grief
and genuine sorrow. There was joy, but it was
of that kind whose exterior is deeply shaded. For
some reason, our approach toward the house had
not been observed by the inmates; and I stood in
the sitting-room before my mother's eye rested upon me. She pressed me to her heart amid tears
and sobs, and for several minutes the silence was
that of death, broken only by convulsive sobs from
all. At length, chiding herself, she began to take
off my wrappings, amid kisses, caresses, and frequent ejaculations of, "Oh, I am so glad you have
come." She took me to the lounge, and once more
my head was resting on my mother's pillow, as in
the happier days of my early life. And now, as
if recalling the note of Mr. Knight, she almost
frantically exclaimed, "My boy, are you blind?
Are you really blind?" From the nature of the
note, she got the impression that I could not

see, or at most scarcely see. I assured her that
for aught I knew my eyes were as good as when I
left home. With this comforting assurance, she
left my side and resumed her preparations for
dinner. The dear sisters and Willie were very devoted, and offered a thousand tokens of their fervent love, anticipating every want and meeting
every desire with much love.

Soon the express-wagon drove up to the door,
and two men came into the room bearing my chest.
At the sight of this my mother exclaimed, " Thank
God, my dream is literally fulfilled." It seems
that a few evenings before she had dreamed of
my return, and that following me two men bore
a chest into the house. The actual scene was an
exact copy of the dream, even to the appearance
of the chest and its bearers. Personally, I entertain great confidence in this particular method of
God's guidance. Of course, the great bulk of
dreams have no reference to the realm of one's future. "Your old men shall dream dreams, and
your young men shall see visions," has ever been
an occasional order of Providence, as has been il-
lustrated in the experience of Jacob, Joseph, Dan-
iel, Peter, and others of Bible times; and the
prophecy of Joel leads to the hope that in modern
times these methods shall have more general favor
with God. Many ministers of modern times, and

many other pious people, have been led and comforted by dreams, which, as they felt sure, have had literal fulfillment, as had this of my mother. We think we might present an interesting argument bearing upon this question did it not seem to us out of place.

The chest was now unpacked, and my wardrobe displayed, which greatly astonished my mother. My father now placed my belt of money in my hands, which I at once poured into the lap of my mother. This, too, astonished her, and she exclaimed, "This, indeed, is a God-send to us." During much of my absence my father had been in poor health, and was thus unable to earn much beyond a bare and plain support for his family. Their circumstances were therefore of the humblest kind; and besides, from continued sickness and pressing wants, they had got somewhat behind with their accounts. It pleased me that this gave them joy; and it lifted somewhat the deep weight of my guilt. At the dinner-table I found every little comfort that a dear mother, from a somewhat scanty larder, could provide; and as with the family I gathered at the board I felt ready for the prayer of thanksgiving. It was a feast fitting for one more worthy than a returning prodigal. However, my heart was too full as yet to eat largely, and my sense of guilt too great to admit of perfect ease.

My coming brought so much joy that I could now see the immeasurable grief my willful and wicked absence had caused. I wanted to confess myself a great sinner at once; and had I done so the word of free and full forgiveness would have been spoken, and I should have had great relief. But for some reason I did not get courage to do so.

My parents, of course, had been exceedingly anxious, having had, as already intimated, no information of my whereabouts or continued existence on earth. They would have had some relief if they had received the letter I placed in Mr. Clark's hand in Boston; but neither this nor any other word had ever reached them. From the moment I left Boston, as the reader will see, I was cut off from every communication with my folks. Many a time I would have written to them had the opportunity offered. Several days passed before the story of my adventures had been fully told to my interested and astonished listeners. A thousand questions were asked, and as many expressions of sympathy were bestowed. I began to feel myself the hero of a strange tale. It seemed impossible to me that I had passed so strange a life and endured and seen so much. My account of Mr. Clark and Captain Sourbier drew from my parents earnest expressions of indignation, while for Mr. Watson and Captain Thomson warmest commen-

15

dations and grateful blessings escaped them. I
wish that in that hour these benefactors could have
received the blessings of my parents, or even those
of my sisters and brother. I think they would
have felt sure that their love and devotion were
not in vain, while the dear sisters of charity, of Rio
Janeiro would have been loaded with benedictions
could they have been reached with words. Many
old friends called to see me, to whom my strange
adventures had to be recounted, but ever with the
members of my own family as interested listeners.
Dear Willie ever clung to my side, and read again
and again the story from my lips

Meantime a letter came from Dr. Morris, of
Philadelphia, containing blanks for my signature,
preparatory to admission to the institution for the
blind, and full explanations, etc., for my parents.
I had told my folks nothing of my intended plan,
and therefore the letter was a great surprise to
them. They said nothing to me about it, but replied that for the present they could not spare me
from home, and should do everything possible for
my comfort. Meantime I was wondering why I
heard nothing from the doctors, and had almost
concluded that their appeal in my behalf had failed. But now another letter came, more urgent
than the first, and I was consulted upon the matter.
My folks so remonstrated that it was concluded to

defer the entrance to the institution for a time at least.

Some six weeks had elapsed, when one day, all of a sudden, I was taken with excrutiating pain in my eyes. I was at once placed under the care of a physician, who directed me to be placed in a room perfectly darkened. The light was excluded by heavy blankets, both from doors and windows, so that nothing could be seen within. This condition continued some four weeks, during which time my mother scarcely left my side by day or night; and most of the time my father was also present with me. Never did a child have more faithful care or more devoted attention. How fortunate for me that I had arrived at home, and to my mother's arms. On shipboard I must have suffered more, and doubtless have died. But God had spared me the affliction until I was prepared for it. Oh, that then I might have more fully appreciated the fact.

Dr. Andrews, the pastor of the family church, often called; but for some reason I ever felt as though there was a chasm between us, over which he could not pass to reach me. Possibly he was too formal in his approach; and perhaps I was too far away in sin and guilt. Still, I was full of good resolutions, deeply penitent, and indeed almost persuaded to surrender myself fully. But almost, however, was all, and not enough. God was raising me up, and gradually I would recede from his fervent, affectionate hold. My recovery was slow; and little by little the pain diminished and the light, as I could bear it, was admitted. Finally the blankets were removed from the windows, and at last I could see God's earth again, and be taken to another room. Friends began to call and gave their hand and word of cheer, and I felt that I was coming back once more into the light of life. My sight was somewhat impaired; but after a time I could get about nearly as well as usual.

It was now determined, however, that I must go to the institution for the blind, and that the sooner I went the better it might prove for me. Preparatory to my leaving, I went on a visit to an aunt, which I enjoyed much; and then, on my return, preparations for my departure began. My mother's heart was evidently heavy, and many a sigh escaped her as she proceeded with my preparation. I also was loath to leave home; I now began to think it the dearest spot on earth. I felt that now I could remain at home forever, and be content with a father's counsel and a mother's love. Duty to myself and my friends, however, prompted me to take this step without delay. I should not be far away, and any day the home friends could come to me or I could go to them.

CHAPTER XXXI.

AMONG THE BLIND.

Having finally arrived with my father at the institution, I naturally recalled the inquiry regarding it which I had addressed to Mr. Gratz, and also my own forebodings at the time. Surely, thought I, my own fears are being realized at last. As we ascended the steps, sounds of music fell on the ear, and merry voices were heard from many lips within. It seemed like a home of life and happiness as well. This by no means comported with my ideas of blindness. Still, the merry voices that I heard, as I imagined, were those of young men and maidens whose eyes had already been sealed in the deep, dark gloom of unending night, and the music was from those fingers which could not be guided with waking eyes. We entered the parlor, and were received kindly by the prefect, Mr. Charles Burns; and in a few minutes later the principal, Mr. William Chapin, came in and welcomed us. He gave us a brief, general history of the institution, and assured my father that his

son should have every needed attention, and that
if circumstances required he would be called to the
city instantly. My father seemed both relieved
and pleased; and arising to go, he promised to
come to me at call if needed. Commending me
to God, he bid me a tender good-by, and I was
alone again, so far as my family friends were concerned.

I now entered the public office, where I met the
other officers and teachers of the institution, all of
whom greeted and welcomed me with great kindness. In their appearance and general manner
they commended themselves to me on sight; and
I felt that I ought to and could easily feel at home
among persons of such genial, kindly spirit and
presence. While sitting here the dinner-bell rang,
and I was escorted to the dining-room. The rush
of the students, coupled with their general hilarity,
surprised me, especially when I recalled the fact,
which was barely perceptible in their movements,
that nearly every one of the two hundred were
stone-blind. The dining-room I found to be divided into two compartments by a partial partition,
covering the sides but not the center of the room.
One of these was for the gentlemen, and the other
for the ladies. This central station was usually
occupied by either the principal or some teacher;
and during the dinner hour the news of the day

was read aloud, and comments of an instructive and explanatory nature were made for the benefit of the students. This was very edifying to me, and did very much to reconcile me to my new home.

We were well waited upon, and the dinner served, though plain, was substantial and relishable. There were a number of tables in the room, each accommodating some ten or fifteen persons. At my table all were blind but myself; and though my presence in the institution was already known, it was not known to my companions at the table that I was present with them. The conversation in part turned upon me, as it happened, and was somewhat amusing. "I say, Bill," said one, "did you know that we had a new student." "Yes, I have just heard so," was the reply. "Have you seen him yet? Is he black or white?" etc. One or two colored students had been admitted to the work-departments of late, and the feeling of the students was rather severe against them. Prejudice is often most determined among those who are themselves most unfortunate. It would seem only natural that a blind man should give himself little concern over the color of a man's skin; yet, to my surprise, I found wonderful sensitiveness here on that and other points of difference.

After dinner a young Mr. Schoolman, who was born blind, and was now well acquainted with the varied departments of the institution, took me in charge. Nearly blind, I found myself intrusted to the guidance of one wholly blind. The blind was literally being led by the blind; and yet there was no danger of the ditch in this case if I followed him closely. He seemed as familiar with every part of the building, and every step leading to the departments thereof, as I with my own room or my own trunk. He also introduced me to the different students, every one of whom he instantly recognized, often by their step; and all of them he knew by name. The different work-departments were first visited,—the broom and brush shops, and the carpet and matting rooms,—the work of which was briefly and interestingly explained. Here the material was all received in the rough, and yet prepared with little trouble and worked up with ease and real skill. The naturalness and ease of the motions of these men suprised me. I began to think really that sight could be dispensed with after all; and yet it was evident withal that if one could not see for himself, another must see for him. Only within a narrow scope and the most familiar walks could a blind man do or go. But if the blind are dependent on others for sight, so too are we all dependent on our companions in a great variety of ways. No man can wholly guide himself, while we need that God should guide us all. Not more willing, neither, is that one whose heart is full of love to guide his most beloved fellow than is God to guide each and every child of Adam. "By his counsel he will lead us [if we will, even through life] and afterward receive us to glory."

We also visited some of the departments of work on the ladies' side of the institution, and saw them engaged in bead-work, knitting, crochet-work, and sewing. It did seem as though their fingers, in their nimble movements, must be guided by eyes that could see. But no; they were wholly blind. Touch answered for sight, and well did it seem to serve them as a substitute. From the work-shops we visited some of the classes in their recitations, which seemed to me both simple and interesting. We then repaired to the somewhat spacious and really beautiful grounds of the institution. These, though seemingly arranged for the eye of sight, were nevertheless intensely enjoyed by the blind, whose love of beauty, and even of flowers in their fragance and fashion, can scarcely be exceeded in those whose sight is in ripest perfection and power. From the grounds I was led to my room, where, while making a general survey, I was glad to rest for a time. In this room I found eight single beds, conveniently and tidily arranged. Of the eight occupants, none could see but myself,

and yet no one of them needed help from me. If
anything, I was the most dependent one of all.
Two wardrobes were arranged conveniently in
either end of the room, each answering for two
students.

At eight o'clock we were called into Exhibition
Hall, where the evening and morning worship was
celebrated. This consisted of prayer, reading, and
singing; and every student was expected to be
present if possible. Different officers or teachers
led in this deeply solemn and interesting service.

A few general words here regarding the institution and the blind of Pennsylvania and the country
generally may not be out of place, nor devoid of
interest to the reader. Its location is at the corner
of Race and Twentieth streets, and, including the
grounds, occupies one fourth of the entire square.
Where the pupil is able to pay for his accommodations and instruction, there is a charge made of
$300 per year; but in my case all was a gratuity
from the state, which with profoundest gratitude
I acknowledge.

On each Wednesday afternoon the institution is
open to visitors, and an entertainment is given by
the students in consideration of a small fee. This
yields to the managers a fund which is used in furnishing an outfit for the students when they leave.
At the time of my entrance there were two hun-

dred students, which was about the full accommodation of the buildings. The school year continues
ten months, giving the heated term of July and
August for vacation, with another brief respite
covering the midwinter holidays. There is, besides,
a permanent home connected with the institution,
where accommodation is furnished to some fifteen
students. The endowment admits of no further
benevolence in this direction at present, although
a charity of such real advantage deserves and
doubtless will before long receive a much more
liberal provision from either the state or the be-
nevolent.

Applicants are registered for admission, and
have to await their regular time. In 1875 there
were fifty-one persons waiting for admittance, while
the institution was really more than full, 207 being
enrolled. There were fifteen in the home, two of
whom were from China, one from New Jersey, and
the balance from Pennsylvania. The course of
instruction consisted of spelling, reading, writing,
pin-type printing,—by means of which correspondence could be carried on between two blind persons without outside intervention,—arithmetic,—
mental and slate,—geography, maps, etymology,
grammar, dictionary, rhetoric, history, natural history, elocution, English and American literature,
physiology, astronomy, physics, chemistry, logic,

constitution of the United States, mensuration, algebra, geometry, Latin, and calisthenics. Besides, instruction was also given in some handicraft, by which, if necessary, a livelihood might be obtained in after years. Generally, too, from one to two hours per day of manual labor were given. The library of the institution was also quite complete in its line; and to the more advanced it afforded greatest gratification. This library consisted of history, natural history, poetry, selections, fables, etc.

By the report of 1875 it is shown that 26,739 brushes of various forms and 30,955 brooms were made by the male inmates of the institution during the year, and by the female inmates 1,958 pieces of sewing, knitting, and bead-work, of a total valuation of $15,773. The most of these goods were readily sold at the institution, or at their Eighth-Street store.

In 1833, forty-five years ago, there were but three institutions for the education of the blind in the United States, while in 1876 there were twenty-seven in all. This is a wonderful growth, and speaks volumes for the sympathy and philanthropy of our noble nation. Nearly every state has provided for its blind, either at home in institutions of it own, or abroad in those of others. The following American states have institutions for the blind, according to the census of 1870 :   Alabama, Arkansas, California, Georgia, Illinois, Indiana, Iowa, Kansas, Kentucky, Louisiana, Maryland, Massachusetts, Michigan, Minnesota, Mississippi, Missouri, New York, North Carolina, Ohio, Pennsylvania, South Carolina, Tennessee, Texas, Virginia, West Virginia, and Wisconsin.   That of Massachusetts was established in 1829, and was the first of all.   Johnson's Cyclopedia gives a list of thirty institutions for the blind in Europe, the first of which was established in Paris, in 1784, a period of forty-five years before America could boast of a similar home for this unfortunate class. Of this list of thirty, all but five were established before that of Boston, the first American institution.

In 1870 there were 1,767 blind persons in Pennsylvania, which was one to every 1,900 inhabitants. At the same time, there were in the United States 20,320 blind persons.   Up to 1874, Ohio had expended by state appropriations for the blind more than $1,000,000, and had at its Asylum in Columbus 169 pupils, while the number of the blind of the entire state was 870.   The ratio to the entire population was one to 1,370, which is a higher ratio than Pennsylvania presents, as will be seen above.

It might be interesting, did our limits admit, to

continue these general statistics further. We trust this reference may awaken in the reader a desire for improved knowledge of this class of our community, and awaken further sympathy in their behalf. The reader may well be grateful for his continued sight; and when he thanks God for the great multitude of daily mercies he should not forget the record of this almost chief of blessings.

But to return to our story. The next morning I was assigned work in the school-room. Although almost a man, I must take the lowermost seat, and begin with the alphabet. A card of raised capital letters was placed in my hands, and I was directed to learn these without the aid of my sight. I must now read with my fingers, as a preparation for my own gloomy future. After a few days a card of smaller letters was given me to learn. I had great difficulty in mastering the situation; and it seemed to me at first an utter impossibility. The teacher would place my finger on a letter, and then tell me to study its shape and determine its name while he was gone to others in the class. This seemed to me like small work, and yet I could see in it a foundation for the future. Writing and arithmetic were taught us in a similar manner, while history and some other studies were learned by hearing them read. For example, the teacher would read the lesson in history, grammar, or geography several times over, and the next day we were required to tell of it what we could. This was the more enjoyable and less difficult method of instruction. I was soon obliged to guide myself about the building. Though I could slightly see, I found great difficulty in this, and met with frequent falls. These mishaps were much enjoyed by my jovial, though sightless companions.

In the course of a month my studies were broken off by another attack of eye-trouble. The attack was quite as severe as that at home; but from the skillful treatment I experienced, and the perfectness of my accommodations, I did not suffer so severely or so long. I was taken to the infirmary connected with the institution for treatment. The second day after my entrance the doctor told me that it would be necessary to perform an operation on my right eye. I made no objection; neither did I inquire as to the nature of it, or even imagine what it was to be. An anæsthetic was administered to me, which induced an unconscious condition; and when I became conscious, my eye was closely bandaged. For ten days following I was kept close in bed, and none of my companions were allowed to visit me. When at last the bandage was removed, I said to the doctor, "I can not see with my right eye, and it seems smaller than the other." He then explained to me the startling fact of its removal. I had known nothing of the loss, nor, indeed, of the operation performed. It was hoped that the removal of the right might restore partially the left eye; and for a time this expectation seemed about to be realized. It speedily became stronger; and therewith my general strength returned, and I was soon able to be about again.

A Miss Brown, a lady most gratefully remembered by me, was connected with the infirmary as teacher of a deaf and dumb boy; and in many ways she rendered me very special comfort and attention. Not only did she anticipate my general wants, but she also read aloud to me during my sickness, as I was able to bear it, and otherwise displayed a real Christian spirit. Angels of mercy will often cross one's path, as the reader will see I had fully demonstrated; and in the person of Miss Brown I had found one who sent much sunshine into my darkened and fainting soul. Heaven guide her in all her ways; and may every weary soul be as graciously ministered to as the writer has been in his wants.

During the time of my, stay my father had visited me on two occasions; and very often letters came to cheer my heart. Indeed, a letter from home with its love and kiss portions, is ever refreshing to a weary, wandering child.

The end of the term had now come, and for two

months the students could be with their friends. Nearly all would leave, although some were without homes to which they could repair. One such was a friend slightly older than myself, formerly from Wales. It was decided that he should go with me, and be my guest during the vacation. Though most of the students expected to return, yet some did not; and withal, the parting season was one of unusual solemnity. The blind were at home amid a companionship wholly in sympathy with themselves; and they preferred to run together the race of life, and fight its battles shoulder to shoulder. The leave-taking was generally affectionate; and unpleasant disagreements were amicably adjusted, forgiven, and forgotten. Separation sometimes brings estranged hearts nearer; and soul-reunion is often possible only in separation. The events of life are well arranged by Him who knoweth what we are and what we need.

The ride home was much enjoyed, and the country air afforded us an exhilarating feeling. I could not descry the face of those familiar forms of nature along the line which I had so often passed; but the sound of song as given forth in the sweet voices of birds never seemed so full of melody to me as now. As the sight diminishes in intensity, the other senses begin to intensify; and I was be-

16

ginning to realize this fact. Especially is this true with hearing, upon which the blind need so much to depend. Seeing by sound is an expression much more rational than many another extravagant and fanciful form of speech.

On arriving at Doylestown we found my father in waiting with a carriage, and we were soon at the door of my home and by my mother's side. Home presented great changes, though my absence had been but for a few months. Ten years were past since Willie came to us, and now another brother had peeped into our humble home and there taken up his abode. This little stranger I found to be a namesake of the renowned General George B. McClellan. To me he was welcome; and, unlike many precious babes, he was welcome to all the house. A babe was a new thing to us, and his infant spirit bound us back again to earlier years. Baby-life makes all the world young again. Even tottering grandparents feel themselves fresh and vigorous again under the genial smile of a darling babe. Welcome, thrice welcome is this new messenger from God. May his future be one of unclouded bliss. May no deep, dark shadows cover his path, but may he profit by the life of his wayward brother. It is a satisfaction to know that by the misery of our example we may have saved others, or restrained them somewhat in the dangerous ways of life. But if baby was a beam of sunshine to our home, he could only at best give a silver lining to another cloud that had gathered over our home. Willie, the dear, pale boy, had broken his leg, and from his suffering was more feeble than ever. He had hardly life enough for this new trial, and it sapped too deeply the fountain of his energy. It but gave a new impetus to his already hurried march to the grave. He was patient and hopeful that ere our vacation was gone he would be a companion for us; and we needed him much as a guide to our feet. He would have been light for our eyes and a staff for his brother's hand.

In Mr. Griffith, my school-mate, I found a pleasant, genial companion, one toward whom my very soul went out. From his own experience, he knew my want better in some ways than the devoted members of my own household. It is well said that "misery likes company;" and the companionship of misery needs to be of kin to itself, or much the same in kind. He who hath himself buried loved ones can best sympathize with him whose sorrow is the same. My companion was early orphaned, and crossed the ocean to this new world when but a child. He had seen much for a blind man, and had suffered much. His experience differed somewhat from mine, and yet in many ways there was some resemblance. He had plowed the deep, blue sea, and knew what the wrath of angry storm did mean. He was a good talker, and delighted in portraying the lessons of his sad and checkered career. He was a good vocalist, also, and gave us beautiful strains of choice music on the violin and guitar. Thus, as a companion he was refreshing at home and welcomed abroad. We strolled together much during the vacation, sharing in the festivities of several picnics, visited the old neighborhood, and forgot not to visit the Sabbath-schools of sunnier days. I could not readily recognize old friends by their features, but by voice I knew nearly all of them full well. Withal, our home-stay was delightful, and we mourned somewhat when we had reached the revolution of the final week. We would fain have stayed longer in a home now so pleasant and full of sunshine and love. Mr. Griffith, by his beautiful Christian life, had contributed much to the spirit of our home, and to the pleasure of our stay. In his denominational relationship he was a Methodist; and though quiet in his demonstrations, yet he was consistent in his life and faithful to his profession. In my heart I longed to be like him, and seriously thought of publicly professing faith at home, and asking for a place in the church of Dr. Andrews with my parents. But the religious approaches to

my heart were too formal and mechanical, and I
finally concluded that in secret and alone I would
carry out my former resolutions.

CHAPTER XXXII.

GROPING FOR THE LIGHT.

Tne last days of August were reached, and we prepared to return for the new school-year. On my return I added to my studies music, singing, and grammar; and for work, I entered the broom department, from which, however, I was soon transferred to the brush department. In the work-room I gave some two hours a day. The permanent workmen were older than the students, and the associations were far from good. Several of them had been in the army, and stories of army-life were told and heard with special satisfaction, but with little profit.

The rules of the institution required that the students should attend one service each Sabbath, wherever they might choose. I used to avoid doing so very often, spending the time instead in social visits to various parts of the city with my blind companions. Some of these men would go all over the city alone, and without even the help of a cane. These visits proved very disastrous to our morals, and I soon found that I had little pleasure in the company of the better class of students. Beer and ale were now often offered me, and I soon partook of them without compunction. There were many religious young men in the institution, and they supported their semi-weekly prayer-meeting. These I rarely attended, but rather yielded to companions who drew me back from God and good works. This, too, in spite of all that my family and friends had done, and in spite of all that God had done and was doing for my comfort and peace. Yet with all of this recreancy God did not forget nor forsake me, and devoted friends still loved me and hoped for my recovery and reform. To accomplish this end, or as a means thereto, the hand of God was to rest heavily upon me once more. I was struck down, and again carried to the infirmary. It began to appear to me that God would break my stubborn heart or destroy my life in the attempt. I was once more under the influence of Miss Brown, whom I had not forgotten, though I had disregarded her Christian counsel. She was again ready with her kind words and gentle, sisterly aid. My old associates were removed from me, and I felt relieved, and thought I would never want them again. But oh, how little did I know of myself.

Mr. Edwards, a Presbyterian clergyman, called

several times to see me, and administered consolation.

One day a gentleman called to see me, who, after some time spent in general talk, took a Bible from his pocket, and at the same moment asked me if I was a Christian. I sincerely regretted that I had to say I was not. He kindly proposed to read, if I felt no objection—as most certainly I did not. He read several passages pointing to the cross by the way of repentance, and then prayed for me very fervently. I felt deeply convicted and very penitent—though I sought to conceal this fact. He told me that he was a missionary from New York, and would like to present my request for prayers to the Fulton-Street prayer-meeting, of which he told me much. I gladly consented to this; and, promising to call again in a short time, he commended me to God and bid me good-day. Mindful of his promise, he called again in a few days. In conversation he dwelt much upon the brevity and uncertainty of life, and insisted that I surrender myself at once to the Lord Jesus. Again he read God's word, and addressed his throne in my behalf. Arising, he wished me to give God my heart on condition that he would raise me up again. I pledged him my word I would, which promise he followed and nailed, as I felt, with another earnest prayer. I felt better in that I was satisfied with what I had done. I spent nearly the entire following night in prayer, and the next day I was glad to see my strange friend again. Once more he commended me to God in prayer, earnestly exhorted me, and bid me a final farewell. I never saw his face again; and memory fails to serve me with his name for my page of grateful tribute. He did for me his part, and did it well. If I am not saved at last, no fault can attach to him.

Once more I was convalescent, and soon was again able to be up and about the house. I spent much time in Miss Brown's room, and her Christian attention was most cordial and refreshing. I tried to believe that I was accepted of my Savior, but soon dismissed this persuasion in the thought that I must experience a much more marvelous change in my feelings.

Before the holiday vacation my father had visited me and invited several of my fellow-students to spend the time at his home in my company. We arranged the visit with a concert of instrumental and vocal music as a part of our programme. The concert came off accordingly, soon after our arrival at home, at the hall of the court-house, in Doylestown. It was well patronized and highly commended.

During this stay my mother desired me to confess Christ publicly, and be known as a follower of his. She had never appealed to me so fervently before. I told her somewhat of my late experience; that I had formed the resolution to live a Christian, but cared not to make a public profession, and should privately, I hoped, show myself such. Never could there be a more serious mistake in any mortal conclusion. The light might as well seek to conceal its glare, the thunder the echo of its voice, the sea its roar, the winds their fury, or even the sun its light. The Christian *must* be known; he *will* be known. To smother the religious fires is to burn up the hope of the soul and effectually wean the heart from Jesus. The hope of acceptance in the morning of eternity is based on the willing and bold confession of Christ before men. Reader, would you be a Christian? Confess Jesus at once, and like a brave warrior rank yourself alongside the followers of the Nazarene. Never did Satan weave a more complete mesh for the feet of the disciples of our Lord than the protestation of my heart to my mother: "I will be a Christian, but the world need not know it."

The day of our departure came again; and this was the saddest leave-taking I ever had with my mother. I am sure I loved her better than ever; and by her simple talk of Jesus she had taken a new hold on my heart. I had, also, some fearful forebodings of the future, which added to the grief of separation. The world was not all dark yet, but I knew not how soon it would be. That ultimately such would be the case, I had good reason to believe; and that the midnight gloom would soon set in, I had almost positive assurance. Should I ever again behold my mother's face, and from the radiance of her eye gather new inspiration for my life? This was a question to which I feared a negative answer must come; and so it proved, in the inscrutable providence of God. *I was never again to see the mother that gave me life.* I should press her hand and catch her words of tender love, but I should never, never more see the face of my devoted mother. If in that parting hour and in the moment of that good-by kiss I had known that her face would henceforth be forever veiled from my sight, surely my heart must have broken within me. In God's goodness, the worst was not known, and I was spared a sorrow that I scarcely could have borne.

My sister returned with me, to wait upon the door as usher of the institution. This was a wonderful satisfaction to me, and softened greatly the bitterness of the pang of parting. But my old friends came around me as of old on my return. They knew of my promises and my serious purposes, and at once they rallied me as a Methodist. I could not endure so much as this for Him who had endured everything for me. However, had any one at this time taken me to their heart in an earnest, Christian manner, I could have stood my ground. But there seemed to be no one thus inclined. Had the situation been clearly understood, I am sure the disposition to support me would not have been wanting. My Christian mates, perhaps, had not that degree of confidence which their kinship to frail and simple humanity should have inspired; and this is a too general mistake with Christians. The seed sown in my heart proved but a wayside seed, having no depth of earth. I forgot my vows, turned my back again on God, and followed my old companions into the ways of sin. I continued until February at my work and studies, and faithfully followed, meantime, my doubly blind guides in all their ways of sinfulness and folly.

Sharp pains now began to attack my remaining eye, and for its examination and treatment I was taken to Will's Infirmary, near by. I was told that an operation was imperative; and I knew too well what this meant now. I refused my consent, and returned to the home. The trouble daily increased, and began to be more than I could endure. Again I went to Will's Infirmary for further examination. I was informed that the eye must be removed. I protested that I could not give up the little sight that I had; I could not part with my last and only eye. "You had better part with your eye than your life," said the professor. Again I refused, and was conducted homeward with a doubly heavy heart. My mother had pleaded with me to never submit again to an operation without first consulting her. She had a horror of the thought that her son should be blind forever. She had said much to me of the horrible darkness of a final blindness; and most surely my own soul recoiled therefrom. The little sight I had was a great help by day; and in the night I could easily follow the light of the street-lamps. A few rays of light were left me in my weary way. The moon could yet rejoice my heart, and the sun was not quite gone down. What wonder that my soul rebelled against the putting out of these lights forever!

There was no abatement to my suffering. It seemed to me that my brain would be crazed, and thus my mind lose its light forever, if I still persisted in clinging to that of the eye. For ten long, weary days and nights I endured the pangs of torment. In this condition I was to decide whether I would exchange light for darkness, day for night. I finally consulted with Mr. Capp, a teacher of the institution and a Christian gentleman. He advised the operation, and said that he would accompany and comfort me in every way possible. Another student was going for the same operation, and I would not be alone. There is a relief in companionship, even when going to the gallows. Sympathy seems to divide suffering and invigorate the soul for its endurance. My reflections were most serious. The condition of blindness was awful to my imagination, and yet I failed in that hour, by far, to take in the full reality or measurement of the dreadful state. I was looking only upon the picture of the coming storm; but I saw enough. Had I seen more, or even half the truth, my soul would have shrunk from contact with the death of darkness, and given itself a victim to the grave of despair. I was forewarned that the operation might be fatal, as in many another case it had been. I had no gold or silver to bequeath, and no houses or lands to will away; and yet I had a soul, the value of which could not be measured by such terms. I knew that I was wholly unprepared for such a fate, and I also knew that that most desirable of preparations was an actual possibility. These serious reflections, however, did not determine me to make the needful preparation; and as I was I went forth to the institution for the operation.

CHAPTER XXXIII.

BLIND AT LAST.

Two days were spent in dieting, before the operation could be performed. The body, if not the soul, must have its preparation. The one was insisted on far more than the other. At last the horrible suspense was over, and the dreadful day come. Some sixty students were assembled to witness the operations, which were conducted by Prof. Morton. My friend, Mr. Overton, preceded me to the operating-room, which was simply across the hall from my room. I was left alone. Though a Christian young man, Mr. Overton feared greatly that the operation might prove fatal. When finally under the influence of the anæsthetic, he imagined himself dead and in the other world, where he was tormented by fiends. I heard with agony his groans, cries, and screams, and my very soul shuddered within me. Dr. Palmer, fearing I might be terrified, came in to pacify me. I really told him I was not terrified; but the deep measure of my terror he must have seen. Fear is instinctive

with all; and by no system of training may the
soul rid itself of this emotion. Its expression is
condemned as unmanly; and thus the soul is driven
to shield its honor behind the veil of deception.
This has been too often done upon the threshold of
the grave and the boundary-line of eternity. This
sentiment of the human heart needs correcting.
Even the agony of Christ in the garden was no
matter for concealment or excuse. He stood in the
deep, dark shadow of approaching torment and
imminent death! If the Master wept and groaned,
so may we. If he struggled and agonized, such
emotions are justifiable in us. Nay, this example
is given for our comfort; not that our tears may
be stayed and our groans stifled, but that the soul
might gather strength for its agony.

The return of Mr. Overton to my room, groaning
and crying, but increased my terror. I felt very
much like receding from my purpose. I had, however, been somewhat hardened to such scenes by
operations that I had witnessed both in the army
and at Rio Janeiro. I was led into the operating-
room with much of the indifference that an ox
would be led to the slaughter. I failed to catch
the first show or sign of sympathy. The surgeon
seems to educate himself against such an expression, as though it were an unmanly sign in him.
Their argument is that life depends on the act, and

thus compensates all suffering, and that any show
of sympathy would but terrify the sufferer to a
greater degree. But the sympathy of the gospel
and its Christ gives birth to an army of heroes and
martyrs such as the world has never seen outside
the church. Why, if sympathy is so desirable and
effective in the one case, is it undesirable and in-
effective in the other? Surgeons, even, may have
more sympathy without any perceptible diminution
of their manhood. I was laid upon a table, somewhat resembling a lounge, for the operation. In
this attitude I was compelled to listen to a brief
lecture by the professor to the students, describing
the operation on Mr. Overton, after which the students were directed to come forward and examine
my eye. This subjected me to absolute mental
torture for many minutes. I was in the condition
of the criminal, who is obliged to listen to the
death-warrant before hanging. This suspense
was horrible, and to my mind wholly unnecessary.
It may have been an advantage to the students,
and possibly for future suffering patients; but I
was in no condition to appreciate the wisdom thereof, and by no means so disinterested as thus willingly to be tortured for the relief of others.

Finally ether was administered to me. It seemed as though my lungs were being filled to exclude
the air therefrom. My hearing became painfully

17

acute. The least sound was almost like that of thunder. The roaring in my head resembled the noise of a fast train continually crossing another track at right angles. The sensation was most horrible. I knew the doctor's hand was on my breast, and that thus he was watching my respiration. He raised my arms and let them fall upon my breast. I felt him use an instrument upon my eye for its exposure, and watched with alarm for the cutting of the knife. But instead, he called to "John" for more ether. Covering the sponge with a cloth, they placed it again upon my face. It seemed now that some one was tearing my throat, and I kicked and struggled violently. Then they strapped my limbs, both legs and arms, that I might have no liberty whatever. Intense suffering followed, but I could not locate it. The horrors of death seemed taking hold upon me; and, literally, I was passing from the world of light to that of darkness.

With my first consciousness I began to wonder where I was, and struggled to get free; but I was yet bound. A terrible pain darted from my eye and flashed over my system. I awakened as one from a midnight slumber in which some horrible dream had disturbed the soul. But then, as now, I could not comfort myself that all was a dream, and that the downy couch was really my refreshing

bed. I knew I was still on the table, and feared
instantly the further operations of the keen, mer-
ciless knife. But the knife had already done its
work. The horrible reality had come at last; *I
was forever blind.*

I was borne to my room by my nurses, who congratulated me for my bravery. Their compliments
were cold comfort, and not highly appreciated. I
was laid upon my bed in a state of extreme ex-
haustion. Mr. Overton was still groaning, though
in his case consciousness had not yet returned.
The suffering was now most intense. It seemed
as though hot irons were being forced into the
socket of my eye. The night was one of agony,
despite all that could be done. Sleep departed
from me, and I felt that I was about to pass through
the gates of eternity. The storm was wild without, as if the very elements were inclined to mock
my grief. The groans of the patients in the ad-
joining rooms, the cat-like tread of the nurses,
together with the beating pacings of the watch-
men on the walks below, all added to the gloom
of the midnight darkness that enshrouded me.

At last the morning came, the patients began to
rise and move about, and the breakfast-bell summoned them for their repast. Their talk annoyed
me, and every simple sound was painful. The day
was a most lonely one, and I longed for my moth-

er's presence with almost every moment. That
my sister did not come from the home seemed more
than strange to me. No one came to see me save
the nurse, and he but occasionally, to see if I had
a want. My suffering was unabated during the
day, and so intense that I could not think of food.
It was tenfold greater than that attending the first
operation.

Mr. Capp called in the evening and brought
sympathy from the boys, who had learned something of my severe suffering. He said my sister
had called, but was not admitted. He sought to
cheer me, and expressed the hope that I would be out
again and back to the home in a few days. This
was really contrary to my expectation, for I thought
I could not survive any length of time. Before
leaving he promised to send me Alfred Nesmith,
a Christian young man whom I desired to see.
Mr. Nesmith had once urged me to become a
Christian, and I felt that now I could appreciate
such talk. I purposed to unburden my whole
heart to him, and hoped he could bear my case
effectively to the Savior. The nurse had overheard the conversation between Mr. Capp and myself, and as soon as he was gone came in and told
me that I must not expect to see Mr. Nesmith or
any other person for several days, as the doctors
had strictly forbidden company.

No one now came near me for several days, and meantime, although my physical suffering was abating, my mental agony was increasing. I felt that I was shut out from the world and from God. In the way of food, nothing furnished me tempted my appetite, and I was sensibly sinking with each day.

One morning I recognized the voice of Dr. Palmer, and I asked him if he was the Dr. Palmer that used to be at the Episcopal Hospital. He was the same man, as I supposed; and after a little conversation he recalled me to mind. He inquired about my appetite, and I told him that I could not eat what I received. The doctor then kindly ordered the nurse to bring me oysters, broiled lamb, toast, etc., saying that he would meet all expense from his own purse. From this time the fare changed, and my appetite improved, with most encouraging results.

One day a gentleman stole to my bedside and said, in a low voice, "Is not your name Smith?" "Yes," said I. "Were you a drummer-boy in the 104th Pennsylvania?" "I was," I answered, with an interest already aroused in my strange friend. "Do you remember Frank Land, of that regiment?" he asked. "Indeed I do," said I. "Well," says he, "I am he;" and he grasped my hand most cordially. I was heartily glad to meet this dear

old comrade. Said he, "I will do anything for
you;" and he faithfully kept his word, proving
himself a most cordial friend in those hours of
need. He took the place of my nurse, and brought
me many a delicacy from the street. He was a
rainbow of light in my dark and cloudy sky.

Mr. Nesmith improved the first opportunity to
call, and said, "I understood you wish to see me."
My heart was full, and yet in the moment it partly
failed me. I wanted to tell him all my grief, and
that sin was the chief reason for my sorrow. I
finally said, "I am not satisfied with myself spir-
itually, and I wish to see a minister." He promised to send me his pastor, a Presbyterian clergyman.

In the evening Mr. Capp came and read to me
from the Bible, and from Bunyan's "Pilgrim's
Progress." The account of the pilgrim in the
slough of despond, I felt, exactly described my place;
but how to get out was the great question. I fear
I was looking for a human hand to help me out.
Mr. Capp, however, spent several hours, and did
much to cheer and console me.

Next morning the Presbyterian clergyman
called to see me. He showed me my condition,
and tried by exhortation and prayer to point me
to Jesus. Still, I felt that he was not approaching
me with sufficient sympathy, and that he could

not help me. Now I longed for the old missionary who had carried my case to the Fulton-Street prayer-meeting the year before. I felt as though his warm sympathy would touch my heart and help my case. Or, could I see my mother, I felt that to her I could freely open my heart. But my mother did not come; and why, I knew not. My sister came at last, and the students and teachers called; but I felt that I wanted my mother more and most of all.

After many days the bandage was removed from my eyes, and I felt that I must certainly see the faintest light. But no; all was darkness. I had entered upon that monotonous night that should end only with my life. In the evening it should be light; and at the death-hour my vision should be restored by the touch of the Son of God. No light to me for evermore, until that great day.

CHAPTER XXXIV.

BACK TO THE INSTITUTION.

I now improved so fast that the doctor consented to my return to the institution. My sister came for me, and by her help I took that sad first walk beneath the sun which should never again cheer my way. My steps were heavy from my weakness, but my heart was heavier from my sorrow. The streets were full of busy life, and the sun was warm and bright; but all were shut out from me. I felt that I no longer belonged to that world into which I was born. I would have felt content to be shut out from the light for a few weeks, months, or even years; but that I should be in deep, midnight darkness *forever* seemed a burden, a punishment that I could never bear. Life had never before been so utterly stripped of its charms. Oh, how my soul longed to break its shackles of everlasting night, and be forever free from the suffering body.

After arriving at the institution I threw myself upon my bed, and spent a long time in a flood of tears. I had not until now given up to my feel-

ings. I had never before fully realized that I was
blind. My walk amid the burning rays of the
sun and the whirling, exciting life of the streets
had made the fact a horrible reality. The orphan
girl's lament, " I am blind; oh, I am blind!" came
to my mind vividly. Mr. Chapin and others called
to encourage and console me. They told me that
I would soon be well, and would be able to get
about among the boys better than ever. But I
was inconsolable. I felt that with my sight, health
was gone, and that I should pine away and die.
The minister called, but I felt myself unable to
bear his words.

My physician advised my return home, inasmuch
as it would be a long time before I could resume
my studies. Why my mother had never visited
me since the operation, no one had explained, and
I feared to ask. However, I was now going home,
and should soon know. My ride home was a most
lonely one. I was alone, and was making my first
journey as a blind man without a guide. On arriving at home I was surprised to find that my
mother and the baby were not present. I could
hear the voices of father, sister, and brother, and
share in their attentive love; but where was mother? In my exhausted condition I feared to ask.
I thought, "She may be sick, or, possibly, she
may be dead." But now my sister astonished me

in her explanation. "Where did you leave mother?" she asked. "Mother!" says I; "I have not seen her." The family had not been apprised of the operation. But my sister had a few days before informed my mother that I was very low; and the morning that I had started for home she had departed for the city. I had thus passed her on the road. But she could not return before the morrow. The physicians had forbidden the communication of a knowledge of my condition to my folks, fearing that I could not survive the shock of their coming. From my wearing glasses, and going directly to bed on my arrival home, my folks had not noticed the fact of my perfect blindness. The next day my mother was at my side; and as she had learned all in the city, it was not necessary that any explanation should be made by me. Through streaming tears she chided me for consenting to the removal of my only eye. I consoled her by saying that I had submitted only as a final and last means of saving my life. My father was deeply agitated over a knowledge of my state, and regretted that I had gone to the institution.

In my personal history I have now reached the latter part of the winter of 1867. I remained at home some two months, until the weather became somewhat milder, sharing, meantime, the best and most careful attention of a mother's loving heart.

The terrible change in my condition, which was somewhat like going from the sunlight to the dungeon, greatly prostrated me, and induced suffering both of a mental and physical nature. But with love and care these disadvantages were finally overcome, and I felt ready to return once more, and for the final year, to the institution. I returned more for the purpose of completing my trade than for further study. I entered the brush department, determined to devote myself carefully to this one branch of business, that I might as soon as possible return to my father's home, both for my comfort and their satisfaction. I gave only some two hours a day to study, dividing my time between reading, writing, and arithmetic, branches which would be to me of practical utility.

The time passed pleasantly, and the summer vacation was soon upon us; indeed, before I felt really ready for it. I had made good progress in my chosen craft, but did not feel myself sufficiently qualified without a few months of further instruction. When vacation arrived I took a well-selected stock of institution work to my home, for sale among the people. As before, a young friend accompanied me and shared with me in my sales and profits. We met with fine encouragement in our sales, disposing of nearly our entire stock. I began to feel somewhat lifted up from the valley of extreme dependence in which I had so long remained by the thought of contributing to some extent toward my own support. Toil sweetens life; and this is no trifling part of the compensation of labor. One's bread is much more palatable for the sweat of the brow and the labor of the hands; and if it is a curse, which we greatly doubt, it is transformed by a gracious Providence into a precious blessing. To the man whose hands are hardened by labor life is less irksome and burdensome, less a valley of darkness and more a mountain of joy, than to him whose unfortunate independence lifts him above humble service and daily toil. The palatial halls of the noble may reflect the glory of art, and their walls may echo with the finest artistic strains, while reveling and feasting may daily yield the soul rich transports of pleasure; yet the poor man's cot holds the larger measure of real bliss and hallowed content. If wealth may give *more* pleasure than poverty, yet the most joy and real, solid bliss is to be found *in* poverty rather than *in* wealth. An even exchange with the rich would be attended with actual sacrifice on the part of the poor. The medium lot is best suited to the want of man; and were we wise, we would more generally pray with Solmon, " Give me neither poverty nor riches."

I now felt more anxious than ever to complete

my trade, that I might command a competency for myself, and by my labor meet my own want. With this end in view, I was not sorry when the vacation months were gone, and when, with my companion, I could turn my face for the final time toward the institution. A few brief months sufficed for this; and obtaining an outfit both of material and machinery, for which I was largely indebted to the benevolence of the institution, I parted company with my old and dear friends. I reluctantly took the parting hand of my companions. I was in a little world, each member of which could give me sympathy such as those who knew not the ways and wants of the blind could not give. Proper and adequate sympathy can come only from mutual suffering. When the young mother stood over her dead child many friends called to express cordial sympathy, and each said and did what she could; but when that mother came whose sorrow and experience was the same as hers, she exclaimed, "Now I have found the friend I want."

The teachers and officers of the institution, too, had endeared themselves to my heart; and it was hard to bid them farewell. No institution could be more fortunate in the selection of its directors than the Pennsylvania Institution for the Instruction of the Blind; and had they been chosen with reference to the comfort and happiness of the inmates, better selections could not have been made. I owe them much, and wish to each not the blessing of my lips only, but the benediction of God.

CHAPTER XXXV.

APPROACHING THE VALLEY.

In company with a young gentleman by the name of Dunn, I returned to my home, where we formed a partnership for the manufacture of brooms and brushes. We obtained a building near my father's door, which we fitted up for our shop, and entered heartily and at once into business relations. Mr. Dunn was a fine workman, and thus was an advantage to me in the direction of personal improvement. For our wares we had a ready market in the surrounding stores, to which we sold mostly at wholesale rates.

My partner was also a good violinist, and had, besides, a general knowledge of music; and from him I also soon learned to handle the violin with considerable skill. This, as a matter of personal cheer, was of special advantage to me. I took great comfort with it in the solitude of home. The music created by my own fingers seemed to feed my very soul, and gave relief in those darker seasons of sorrow and despondency. But that which God intended for a blessing was trans-

formed by human influences into a snare and a
curse. My nature was too easily aroused and too
responsive to the quick and lively strains of the
strings. My violin became a stone of stumbling
to my feet, and was the blind guide which too
nearly led one poor blind man into the yawning
pit and the jaws of cruel moral death. I have
no voice of condemnation for the instrument; for
even now my soul loves to be awakened from its
chilling dreams by its inspiring strains. But no
instrument so besets the feet of mortals with mur-
derous temptations, and none has won for the evil
one so large a harvest of precious souls. A number of years ago a young violinist was brought to
Christ; and he immediately asked his minister,
"Shall I cast away my violin?" "No," said his
minister, "but be careful in the selection of your
tunes." This is an important matter, and one so
difficult to control that often the violin had better
be laid aside. At least it is not wisdom for the
child of God to nestle in his bosom a viper that has
poisoned so many with his venomous sting.

I had now become considerably reconciled to
my condition, and found that complete blindness,
at least in my case, was far better than partial
sight with constant suffering and ill health. I
found that even a blind man was by no means excluded from the world of light and happiness, and

that from the increased acuteness of touch and hearing the dispossession of sight, though an immeasurably great affliction, could be borne. As

"Darkness shows us a world of light
We never see by day,"

So blindness gives acuteness to the powers of imagination, which makes it a fruitful realm for the soul. The world knows not how much it owes to the blindness of Milton; for it is certain that with continued sight "Paradise Lost" would never have been written by him, as other duties would have claimed his time and skill. It is quite evident, too, that with his sight his imagination could not have produced it. Nor must it be forgotten that Homer, whom common consent places at the highest pinnacle of poetic excellence, notwithstanding the great antiquity of his age,—eight hundred years before Christ,—was shut out from the light of the world by blindness. Handel speaks of two celebrated musicians that were blind. From under the cover of blindness many sweet voices have spoken words; and hands undirected by sight have performed deeds which have cheered and electrified the universal family.

My brother Willie was a constant companion for me, and administered to my wants in a thousand ways, and with tenderest love. My parents now seemed content, in that I was so near to them,

18

and in that they could extend to me their watchful care. Very many came to our home, drawn
largely by the curiosity of the work of blind men,
so that it was hardly ever a place of solitude or
gloom. For myself, I loved company better than
ever; and though I could see no face, yet I could
not bear to be alone for even the briefest time.

My partner proved anything but an advantage
to me in many ways. He had been raised a Catholic; and though devoted theoretically to that faith,
yet he was not largely restrained by it in a moral
way. He was an inveterate smoker, and occasionally used the flowing bowl to excess. He was also
very fond of light company; and companions of
this kind were often and much of the time in our
shop. Parties, too, were the delight of his soul,
and to these, in company, we often repaired. Of
course, the violin was not forgotten by either of us;
and until the midnight hour, and often until the
gray light of morn was near, we measured time
for the giddy trip of the fantastic toe. My conscience struggled against this course of conduct as a
great impropriety, and my parents were faithful in
their protestations and warnings. I had not forgotten the resolution of the year before, to lead
and live a religious life, and really fancied much
of the time that I was in fact accepted of God. I
would attend church with great regularity, but

mostly as a mere matter of form. My soul did not enter into the worship of the sanctuary, though my feet wended their way into the consecrated house.

My parents saw that my companionship was not suited to my want, and that my partnership with Mr. Dunn must be terminated. This was a difficult thing to do. From my heart I felt a profound interest in, and no small friendship for him. With sight, I might never have chosen such a companion; but in our mutual blindness I could unbosom my soul to him with a surprising familiarity and a real confidence. He could in many ways answer my wants better than almost any other, because my condition was better understood by him. But his habits of dissipation were growing upon him; and, as a consequence, his spirit was losing its usual amiability. He became a trouble to my parents, and brought clouds of sorrow over our home. At the end of a year our partnership was dissolved, and my companion went forth into the world alone. Shortly afterward he met with an accident which disqualified him for work, and the alms-house became the home of my old, blind friend.

Although my companion was gone, the violin was left behind; and the old habits he had helped me to form were not to be easily broken. The hilarious comrades which the instrument had drawn about us were still often with me, and persisted on my continued attendance with them. Too often, for the cheer of their company and the trifling compensation they gave, I would join their parties and contribute to their unreal joys. This companionship continued for some two years, during which time the tendency was unmistakably downward. The violin, although affording me sweetest possible music, was leading me slowly but steadily and surely downward into the valley of deeper darkness and certain moral death.

In the providence of God, a change of location was determined on by my father; and though the distance was but a mile, yet it threw me into another and in some respects better neighborhood. It took from me largely my old social companions, and led me to depend more exclusively upon the single and blessed companionship of Willie, who in his devotion was faithfully seconded by the other home friends. My mother, as she was able, became my companion in the work of the shop, while Willie also assisted in a variety of ways. He also became the salesman of my goods, and thus entered into a partnership of the profits.

My sister had left the institution at the time of my return home, and for two years our family had been unbroken. But changes were soon to trans-

pire, and the family circle was to be broken forever. My oldest sister had consented to marriage with a gentleman of Philadelphia, a Mr.
McGargle, with whom she soon after removed to
her city home. In the following year another
change was to come; another link was to be taken
from the family chain. The festivities of a wedding were to be followed by the solemnities of a
death and the horrid gloom of a burial. My dear
brother Willie, in whom my soul was delighting,
was gradually but surely failing, and it was evident that the dear boy could not long remain with
us. From the thought of his death, however, my
very soul recoiled. He was eyes to his blind brother, and a willing, loving guide for my weary feet.
But we must not anticipate too much.

Upon this sea of gloom let us drop the curtain
for a time. Anticipation brings sorrow before its
time; and too often we court the immediate presence of misery, when in truth it is a long way
off. Until the darkness comes let us walk in the
light, and cheer our hearts with the music of the
present.

I had now become thin and worn by close confinement; and I longed to get out, both for a change
of labor and the fresh air of heaven. A newspaper
advertisement for book-agents was read to me. I
at once entered the service of the house, and by

the help of a boy canvassed the surrounding country.   This business I followed during the warm season with special advantage to my health, and good
pecuniary profit.   In bad weather, and for rest, I
would occasionally spend a few days in the shop;
and when winter came I gave my full attention to
brush-making.   During my summer rambles I did
not have the companionship of Willie, as he was
not able to endure so much fatigue.   With the
change of weather in the fall his cough became
rapidly worse, and soon he was confined continually to the house.   No more should he lead me
forth, and no more direct my steps.   We had
strolled together for the final time, and our arm-in-
arm pilgrimage had ended at last.

A Mrs. Ford made her home in our house, and
manifested much religious interest in Willie.   One
day she said to me as I sat in her room, "I
fear we are soon to lose Willie.   Did you ever say
anything to him of his future?"   I was saddened
and confused by the solemn confession regarding
my brother, and the question propounded to me.
I said, "I have had no conversation with him; nor
do I feel that I can speak to him of this serious
and awful matter.   I much wish, Mrs. Ford, that
you would do this service for me."   She expressed
a desire to do so, and requested me to bring him
to her room.   Poor child!   I felt that I was to

bring him to a solemn court, and that I was to be
the means of increasing his sorrow. He well knew
that his case was alarming; but whether he had
even thought of dying, I did not know. I soon
had my brother at the lady's side for the sad interview. She talked with us generally about the
other world, and sought in a tender manner to
impress upon us the fact and certainty of death.
She then spoke directly of Willie's condition, and
of the possibility of an early death in his own case.
Verily my heart bled within me for the poor boy.
It seemed almost a cruelty that such words should
be spoken; and yet I felt sure that they were necessary. To my surprise, and my relief also, he
replied to Mrs. Ford, "I love my Savior, and am
not afraid to die." We were all overcome, and
wept in silence. No further words were spoken
then; and no other words needed to be spoken. I
mourned for Willie, and yet I rejoiced with him. He
needed pity less than myself; for he had what I had
not, and that to which I was an unhappy stranger.
Could I have had his preparation, as I felt then, I
would have gladly exchanged my condition for his.
Further frequent and extended talks were had with
Willie by Mrs. Ford, in which, though I did not
participate, my soul had a joyful share. If we
ourselves are unready for the solemn change it re-
joices us greatly to know that our dear friends are

thus prepared. Our very joy over another's preparation but indicates its value and necessity for us.

Dear Willie often inclined to talk with me about heaven and our angel brother on the other shore; but I was in no frame of mind to encourage such conversation. I repelled the dear boy, and sought to turn his thought and talk in other ways. I rejoiced, nevertheless, to see his perfect reconciliation, and did not doubt his complete preparation for the solemn ordeal of death and the glories of the other life.

The confinement within doors was speedily followed by close confinement to his bed and the reduction of his frail form to a state of complete emaciation. We were often called to his bedside to witness what we feared would prove the actual approach of death. At last the cough ceased, and the doctor warned us that now the end was near, and that at any day or hour the dear child might go forth to the unseen though not distant clime. A night of semi-unconsciousness, of a kind which usually precedes death, now came upon Willie, and we were all silently watching in expectation of his momentary departure. The night without was wintry, wild, and cold, a night in which death would clothe itself with more than usual gloom. He was lying restlessly upon the lounge, and mother, hoping to ease her dying boy, lifted him gently to the bed. Suddenly he aroused opened his eyes, and said, "Mother, I wish to see Mr. Andrews." The doctor had frequently called, and had added much to my brother's peace of mind. But now the valley was near; and though Willie had therein the staff, the rod, and even the presence of God, he would also have his servant near by. It was God, indeed, that divided the waters of the Jordan, and made them stand as a heap above the advancing Israelites; and yet the feet of the priests must first touch these waters before the deed was done. And so, in the providence of God, the presence of his chosen ministers helps even now to divide the waters of death before his advancing and descending children. My father went hastily for Dr. Andrews. Meantime Willie talked much to us all. Mother and the sisters were weeping bitterly, when our dying Willie said, "Don't weep for me; I shall soon be better off. I know I am dying, but I have no fears." Mr. Andrews, on arriving, went to his bedside and took his hand. Willie calmly gave the doctor a message for his Sabbath-school mates. The minister proposed prayer, when Willie said, "Let it be a little child's prayer." After the prayer, he called for me. Advancing, I took the dying brother's hand and whispered in his ear, "Willie, how is it with you?" He replied, "It is well, and I will soon be safe with Brother Ross." A moment's silence followed, after which he reached his hands upward, and said, "Hark! Don't you hear the music?" With these last words, with a countenance lighted up with a smile, and with a slight shiver that but faintly approached a struggle, my brother Willie was gone. The angels had come, he had heard their music, and he had gone to join the chorus of the heavenly song. The silver cord was loosed, the golden bowl was broken, the pitcher was broken at the fountain, and the wheel was broken at the cistern. His hour of departure was a fitting one. The storm had passed, and the light of the sun was coming upon the earth for us as the light of glory broke upon the deathless soul of Willie.

But I could not realize that Willie was dead, though every sign of death was about me. Friends were calling, preparations were being made for the burial, and yet the fact of death was not real to me. I had indeed *heard* the farewell word, but I had not *seen* the soul's departure. I went often to his room, and passed my hand over his cold, silent form, as if to assure myself that he was really dead. I was in awful agony, and yet I could not weep. It seemed to me that the fountain of my tears was forever dried, and that for lack of weeping my soul within me would break. Oh, the relief of tears. They are, indeed, the safety-valves of the heart when too much pressure is put upon them. Thus the full heart of Christ found relief by the grave of Lazarus. Doubtless, too, on many another occasion Jesus found relief in tears. If their Savior wept, well may poor sinners. weep.

At length the hour for burial arrived; and by the side of our now encoffined Willie we sat in sorrow for the funeral service. A brief discourse, a solemn prayer, and we were in our carriages for the final resting-place of the dead boy. The coffin was lowered, a few words of impressive weight followed, and then the friends advanced for the last sad look upon the casket of the dear dead. In this deeply-solemn scene only the eyes of my imagination could join. At last the final word of benediction was said, and Willie was left to sleep beside his brother Ross. Until the voice of God is heard and the trump of the archangel shall sound, their sleep shall be unawakened.

The reader could not know by any words of mine how keenly I felt the death of my brother Willie. As an affliction, his death was next to the loss of my sight. I felt, indeed, that my eyes had been newly put out, for the dear boy was eyes to me. He who stood nearest to my own heart in all my ways had fallen at my side. And yet, possibly, in the providential training of God, this affliction was a step for my recovery and redemption. Of course it was not a step accomplished *for* that end, and yet one graciously overruled *to* that end. The removal of my father from the old neighborhood, and the departure of my blind companion, had done much for me; and yet Willie, while alive, had been a connecting link with me to my old and gay companions. Taking me forth upon the streets, we would fall in company with them; and often they would induce Willie to go home and leave me with them and in their care. Consenting, I was thus often ensnared; and many long hours of the night I would foolishly contribute to the unreal pleasures of my gay companions. But now that Willie was dead, my last means of reaching this class was gone. I was forced to remain at home, or go but seldom. This made home a somewhat solitary and lonely place to me, and I soon began to grow uneasy.

CHAPTER XXXVI.

SALVATION.

I concluded to canvass again; and going one day to the printing-office, I obtained a good number of exchanges, and with my sister's aid examined the advertising columns. The New World Publishing Company called for agents to sell "Olive Logan's Mimic World," and I at once secured an agency covering contiguous towns. Securing the guidance of a lad, I was soon in successful business, and began to gain handsome dividends beyond my really large expenses. Frequent complimentary letters came from the company; and finally they requested an interview with me. On a specified time their manager, Mr. Vandersloot,—a gentleman who will figure conspicuously in subsequent pages,—called to see me at my home. The kindness and general cordiality of the gentleman favorably impressed me. Another book was placed in my hands for sale, and my territory was enlarged, while Philadelphia became the headquarters and center of my growing business. Mr.

Vandersloot's house became my home when in the city. This was a wonderful favor, and a real advantage to me. I was now general agent; and while allowed a good commission on my personal sales, I also derived quite a dividend from those of my agents. I was personally everywhere kindly received, and sympathy gave me ready and profitable sales.

Mr. Vandersloot gave very strict attention to his business, and would on no account leave his post of duty during his working-hours. He had a strong hold, also, on the fellowship of the Protestant Episcopal Church, of which he was a devoted member. After business hours, however, he sought both relaxation and pleasure; and sallying forth of an evening he would give free play to his mirthful, lively spirits. Nor would he hesitate to enter a respectable restaurant, and, like the German that he was, call for and rejoice in his sparkling lager. I really liked his good nature, and could heartily join in his jovial, hilarious laugh, while his tempting beverage I could accept with special relish. Still, I could not but think this course unbecoming to and inexcusable in one professedly a Christian; and it went very far to neutralize not only my confidence in him as a gentleman, but also his influence over me as a Christian. A trifling act of impropriety will often neutralize the

full power of a Christian life; and hence the necessity of guarding carefully our simplest word and
deed. Mr. Vandersloot himself, as we shall see,
lived to realize the importance of this fact.

Finally, the books that I was handling growing
rather stale on my hands, I concluded to handle
others for a time. I thus transferred my interest
to another house, and bid a present farewell to the
home of Mr. Vandersloot. I was now on the road
more than heretofore, and rarely in the city. I
was generally stopping at hotels, and found my
companionship to be, as a rule, anything but profitable to myself. Several months passed, during
which time I rarely ever thought of my old and
true friend, Mr. Vandersloot. In the fall, however,
I was in the city again, and at my hotel met with
an old, jovial friend of other days. After tea, we
took our cigar and sauntered forth for a chat and
a walk, and finally concluded to turn into the theater. Before separating for the evening we had
fallen in company with another jovial friend; and
together we arranged to attend the theater of the
following evening. After the theater we proposed
to have a specially good time, as the judgment of
the world would determine it. My companions
were both gay, and a brilliant time was anticipated.

In the morning my friend had to leave the hotel
for special business; and being left alone, I hardly

knew how to spend the time. The thought soon occurred to me, however, to hunt up my old friend and helper, Mr. Vandersloot. Accordingly, I took the street-car, and soon found myself at his place of business, where he was, as usual, hard at work. He was now engaged in publishing "The Inspired Life of Christ," a work which presented the Savior's life wholly in Bible language. Though hard at work, he cordially entertained me for the day; but his conversation covered social and business matters exclusively. We dined down town; but at the close of work-hours he insisted that I should go home with him for tea. I at first objected, insisting that a previous engagement made it an actual impossibility; but as he so earnestly insisted, I finally consented to go. And this reluctant decision, in the providence of God, was the pivotal act of my life. Immense and everlasting consequences depended upon that decision and clustered around that moment. To accompany Mr. Vandersloot to his home for tea was to be worth more than the value of a world to me. It was seemingly but a trifle in my way; and yet, as Napoleon remarked, "Men are led by trifles." On another occasion he said, "What mighty contests arise from trivial things." But "trifles make perfection," and "the smallest hair casts its shadow," so that it is not very strange that even the acceptance of an invitation to tea should have given a new tinge to the whole of my coming life. How this was done we are to see.

While we were at tea a Mr. Fox called; and after an introduction I insisted on taking my leave, owing to my engagement. Mr. Vandersloot, however, objected, saying that they were both going down town, and I should accompany them. With great reluctance I consented, and together we started down the street. The cars were passing, and I wondered that no motion was made toward them. I should here observe that in the spirit of Mr. Vandersloot I noticed a remarkable change, the nature of which I could hardly explain, and the reason for which I could not understand. He was still cordial and social in the extreme, but the trifling spirit was gone; and there was a somewhat solemn and very serious expression in his general manner. He had said nothing to me of religion, and nothing of his own religious convictions and life. Still, he felt in his heart an intense interest in my religious well-being; and while longing inexpressibly for my redemption, he determined to make no personal advance, but rather to bring me within the influence of a moral power which I should not be able to resist. There was wisdom in this course, especially in my case; and Mr. Vandersloot presented an example deserving of careful imitation.

19

Theodore Cuyler speaks of a child whose mother, a member of his church, was a binder of shoes. One day this child took work to the merchant from her mother, and ventured to invite him to their weekly prayer-meeting. He promised to attend, and kept his promise. The attendance resulted in his conversion, and in the beginning of a mighty reformation. The little girl led the man to the place where Jesus could meet him. We too often trust in our own mere word, when the soul stands in need of the influence of the altar within the sanctuary. An invitation to the house of God should be the daily salutation of God's children to the wandering, careless sinner. The world is waiting to come to Jesus; but the church is too generally withholding the simple, personal call. God spreads the feast; let us lead our friends thereto, that they may be fed.

Mr. Fox finally inquired of me as to my church relationship, with the thought, doubtless, of leading me into a religious conversation. Mr. Vandersloot, however, had determined on another plan, and relieved me by instantly replying: "Mr. Smith's folks are members of the Presbyterian Church." We now turned from the sidewalk and ascended several stone steps, when we paused. Several persons passed quickly up the steps, and on by us; and I inquired of Mr. Vandersloot, "What place is this?" He astonished me by replying, "This is the Twefth-Street Methodist Episcopal Church." "What is going on here, Mr. Vandersloot?" I asked. "There is a class-meeting here to-night," was the answer. "What kind of a class-meeting?" said I, in utter ignorance· of the nature of such a meeting. "A Methodist class-meeting. Were you ever in one?" said he. On answering that I had never been in such a place, he said, "Well, then, come in for once." "Not to-night," said I; "for, as you know, I have an engagement." "What is the hour of your appointment?" Mr. Vandersloot inquired. "Eight o'clock, at the farthest," said I. "Oh, well," said he, "it is only seven now; come in for awhile." I very reluctantly consented, and went into the house very much confused and abashed, failing entirely to understand this strange conduct of my old Episcopal friend. There were some thirty persons in the room—the ladies arranged on the one side and the gentlemen on the other. The leader opened the meeting, and after prayer related his personal experience. He then called on the ladies in order, from each of whom came a word of personal experience. When I went in I had determined to leave the room as soon as the meeting was fairly opened; but for some reason or other I had lost the direction of the door. For the life of me I could not tell by which direction we had entered the house. In this confusion of mind I dare not start; and a slight spirit of dissatisfaction with the course of Mr. Vandersloot determined me not to ask his aid, so I sat quietly, but for a time in a state of semi-desperation.

However, as soon as the ladies began to speak, and the voice of exhortation was alternated with that of song, I became deeply interested and somewhat seriously affected. I began to see that every one in the room was speaking in order; and the thought that I might be expected to say something threw me into a state of terrible agitation. After the ladies were through speaking the first leader retired from the stand, and an old man took charge of the class. During the most part of his life he had followed the sea, and not until he was an old man had he found the blessed peace of religion. His talk covered his personal experience, and to me it was absolutely wonderful. It charmed me, and took deep hold upon my soul, melting me irresistibly to tears. There were only three men on my right, while Mr. Vandersloot was the first on my left. He said to me in a whisper, "When it comes your turn you must speak." "Oh, no," said I, horror-struck; "I must be excused." "No, sir," said he, "we excuse nobody here; you *must* speak." I was both tried and dumbfounded, and now began to see that I was truly in a moral trap, and one which my peculiar friend had strangely laid for me. The situation seemed an impossible one; and the conduct of Mr. Vandersloot was absolutely beyond the reach of interpretation. Had he been on my right side instead of my left, I should have felt a world of relief; for, most of all, I wished an open door to his soul, and a vision of his moral feelings.

The first man was now speaking, and soon the man next to me had spoken; and after the song, the silence of death began its reign. They were waiting for me; and Mr. Vandersloot, by tender nudging, was reminding me of the fact. But I determined not to move; that the silence should not be broken by me. All eyes were upon me, as I knew; and I burned with shame and confusion. If I would not break the silence, the dear old man would do so himself. He advanced to my side and, placing his hand tenderly on my head, said, "Young man, can you not say one word for Jesus—not one word for Jesus?" It was the voice of a patriarch, and seemed to me like God's own appeal to my soul. It was too much for me; and while it almost broke the heart within me, it also brought me to my feet. I dared not refuse to rise. I felt myself lifted up by a mysterious power. I would hardly now have kept my seat for a world. I made several ineffectual attempts to speak, but my utterance was choked with fear and emotion. But I finally said, in substance, "I am not a Christian; but I hope some time to be, and am fully determined yet to leave the world of sin and flee to Jesus, that when weighed in the balances in the final day I may not be found wanting. Pray for me; I am a poor, needy sinner."

When I requested prayers I supposed only that they would remember me at their homes; and in the thought of thus transferring my case I felt a special relief. But the old man could see through my case clearly, and knew just my want. He proposed to carry toward completion a work so unexpectedly introduced. He saw the condition of the patient, and knew what remedy the case demanded, and that death was sure to follow as the result of its continuance. He addressed some soothing and helpful words to me, as he had done to others who in their experiences had developed special want; but he was not satisfied there and thus to rest his case. That I was brought to an earthly friend, was much; but this earthly friend would bear me in his own arms to the arms of Jesus. "This case," said he, "demands immediate attention;" and down the old man kneeled before me for prayer. Such a prayer I had never heard before, never have I since, nor shall I, indeed, from mortal lips. It was a quiet, earnest talk with God, and for me; a lift heavenward, such as I had never had.

Following this prayer Mr. Vandersloot spoke. He referred to the reluctance with which I came into the church, but now hoped and believed that all of my objections were removed. He thanked God for the first class-meeting he had ever attended; felt sure that in God's hands it had proved the means of his conversion, and hoped it might prove as much of a blessing to me. He referred to his last meeting with me, and to his former general life before me, saying that he could now see that it had not been what it should have been. By this talk I was much moved, and thereby began to get an insight into his present religious nature. But if I was moved by his talk, much more deeply was I affected by his prayer; for he now knelt by my side and offered to God a fervent petition in my behalf. After the other gentlemen had spoken, several fervent prayers were offered specially for me, following which the meeting was closed. We did not leave the house, however, until many cordial, Christian words had been spoken to me by different ones.

I had attended a very strange meeting; and its results had wonderfully surprised me, for they were even unthought of. I firmly supposed I should spend the evening at the theater, and with carousing friends; but God had arrested me in my course —not as he did Paul, but as effectually as he had reached him. With all my confidence in and esteem for Mr. Vandersloot, it is doubtful whether he could have reached or even touched my heart with any personal words during the day. The conversation sought by Mr. Fox on the way to church would perhaps have opened my eyes, or at least have repelled me to my religious hurt. If Mr. Vandersloot had even remotely suggested the idea of spending the evening at a Methodist class-meeting, I should have instantly and stubbornly resisted and rejected the idea. He had reached me by the only route open to my soul; and I hesitate not to say that in all his procedure I believe definitely, and though perhaps unconsciously, he was led of God.

The meeting itself was the religious *modus operandi* that my soul needed for its own proper impression. I had never been in such a meeting; nor had I ever seen such a reflection of human experience or such a beautiful unfolding of the religious life. I saw the beauties of the Christian brotherhood and the sweet glories of the Christian family as I had never seen or even dreamed of them before. I learned that the spirit of religion could subdue the heart of stone and transform the soul of sin as the simple abstract truth and formal theory of religion could not. Several of the sisters had confessed their sorrows and lifted the veil that concealed their troubles from the eye of the world, and the leader had responded in words of comfort and consolation that had refreshed them and edified all. For all time, I was convinced of the utility and moral effectiveness of such a class of meetings, and of such a system of religious and social work. What had proved so great a blessing to me must, I thought, be a special blessing to all.

In my heart I must say I reluctantly left that house of God. If I had gone in with hesitation, I was going forth with greater misgivings. I was now fully persuaded of my want, and yet as fully convinced that that deep want was as yet unmet. On the way home it seemed strange to me that Mr. Vandersloot said nothing of the meeting and made no special reference to religious matters. A few general words only broke the otherwise unbroken silence of the homeward walk. When we arrived at home he took down the old family Bible, and after reading a chapter offered his usual prayer. The fact that he had spent the evening at God's house and had there joined in prayer and praise did not excuse his usual family devotion. He was the priest of his own family, and would not suffer the evening sacrifice to be forgotten or allow the fire to die out upon the altar. In this, too, he gave the world an example that may with safety have imitation.

How strange all this seemed to me, and how this new form of devotion added to my personal conviction. If he had carelessly spent the last hour of evening, or had even gone to his room for rest without prayer, perhaps the work of the Spirit would have been stayed in my case. On retiring, he also proposed to room with me, as he had often done when I was an inmate of his home. Getting to our room, he went directly to bed and was soon asleep. His conscience was at rest, and he was soon reposing in his Master's arms. I did not think of retiring at once, but sat in my chair for meditation. It seemed impossible to make the preparation for retirement. The words, " choose ye this day whom ye will serve," were ringing in my ears, and were before my eyes as though written upon the wall in letters of flaming light. I was crushed under the load of conviction, and was longing in vain for relief. Objections to my contemplated consecration arose in my mind. " What will my young friends say," thought I. " Will it not do for me to lead simply a moral life? If I give up all to Christ now will I not wound the cause by going back again into the world?"

Perhaps Satan never suggested to the sinner a more foolish and sophistical excuse than this last one mentioned. The idea that because a failure would wound the cause of Christ, therefore the attempt toward the Christian life had better not be made! Indeed, better continue heartily in sin for the whole life than to even make an effort to break off one's sins! The crime of backsliding is great; yet it is not so great as the uninterrupted continuance in sin. I would lead a man to Christ if he served him but a month. If for that time only he did not sin, or by the help of God tried not to sin, Satan would meet with some loss, and the soul would make some gain. Even he who can keep down and put back the growth of a weed has done some good, even though he may not wholly uproot it. But whatever one may think of "once in grace always in grace," we confidently think that the cases of actual and complete backsliding, where the soul has really been born of the Spirit, are at least very rare. Even though there be a seeming falling away, the Spirit is apt to finally reclaim its own.

At last I advanced toward the bed, thinking to retire. I but reached the foot railing, and leaning over it it seemed that I could go no farther. It appeared to me that for my soul the last opportunity had come. I must fully surrender now, or perhaps I should never surrender. I determined, while the clock struck two, that I would now and forever be a Christian. Mr. Vandersloot was peacefully sleeping, wholly unaware of the terrible struggle into which, as God's agent, he had thrown my poor soul. I advanced to his side and awoke him. I told him of my distress, and of my purpose. He arose, and we knelt in prayer. We spent a half hour or so in alternate prayer. At last peace came, and the cloud departed. I could *see* for once as I had *never* seen. We retired for rest; and though the night was now short, I was soon in the most peaceful and refreshing sleep I had ever had. In the morning the usual family worship transpired; but no reference was made to the night before and its solemn work, although the family well understood it all. They were wisely allowing the Spirit to do its own work. Mr. Vandersloot took me to his office for the day, and on the way we met Mr. Fox. I frankly told him of the occurrences of the night before, at which he expressed much joy and assured me of his fervent prayers.

Arriving at the office, Mr. Vandersloot related to me a brief and explanatory chapter of his personal experience. A few months before he happened to be in a Methodist class-meeting; and from the warm, cordial spirit of the worshipers,

and the large, rich measurement of their joy, he
was satisfied that they had what he had not, and
yet something that he greatly needed. He left
the place determined on fervent prayer for a further and complete change of heart. He had not
prayed in vain, but had soon found the very change
for which he sought; and that he might·live in
the atmosphere that had begotten the desire for
this change, and give his heart fully to the blessed
work of saving men, he had changed his church
relationship, and united with the Methodists.
Now he felt as though he was working for Christ,
while his life was one of immeasurable peace. His
talk fully sufficed to lift the curtain; and I no
longer wondered at his anxiety for me, nor at the
course he had pursued. If I had had bitter feelings and measurable indignation against the man
eighteen hours before, the bitter feelings were now
sweetened, and the rising cloud of indignation had
given way to a clear sky. If I had condemned, I
now blessed the man, and accepted him as my God-
given benefactor

CHAPTER XXXVII.

AMONG THE METHODISTS.

In the evening we went to Mr. Vandersloot's own church-home,—St. Pauls Methodist Episcopal Church,—where Mr. Welch, the pastor, was holding a series of revival-meetings. He preached a plain, earnest sermon on "The True Foundation or Basis of the Christian Life," at the close of which he invited souls to the altar. I felt that I wanted to be at the altar of prayer; and Mr. Vandersloot led me up among the mourners and seekers. After earnest prayers, several spoke kindly and encouragingly to me; and yet I felt that in spirit, if not in word, they had not what I wanted. Then an old man came to me and said, "My brother, what is your trouble?" His spirit touched me, and I felt to exclaim, "Sir, you are the man I want to talk with." I said, "I have peace, but not feeling enough." Said he, "Trust in God, have faith, believe his promises, press your case in prayer, and feeling will come in good time, as you may need."

His words did me a world of good, and mostly, perhaps, because of the spirit of sympathy in which they were spoken.

It was not the *power* of Christ that drew the multitude, even though that power could restore lost senses, lost health, and, indeed, lost life; but it was the *love* and *sympathy* of Christ. Even yet his love constraineth us. We feel that in him "we have a faithful High-priest, one that can be touched with the feelings of our infirmities. Christ has the fullest confidence of mankind because of this. The world to-day most needs love and sympathy from its fellows; and the power to win men is in these beautiful expressions. A child in Chicago was in the habit of going five miles to his Sunday-school, passing thirty other schools to reach his own. When remonstrated with for the folly of his course, he simply remarked, "They love a fellow over there." Love made his five-mile walk a pastime. In the light of the flame of love men will endure all dangers, and yield their wealth, their stations, and their lives as an offering,

A London clergyman explains how by the light and power of a smile he led an entire family to his church and to Christ. Passing a window one day on his way to Sabbath-school and church, he met the gaze of a sweet child, to whom he ex-

tended a smile. The next Sabbath the same child
was at the window, for whom he had another smile
of love. The third Sabbath there were several
children at the window, on whom he smiled as he
passed. But looking back after passing, he saw
these three children following him. They entered
his church and took their places in his school as
scholars. The next Sunday the parents were at
his place of worship; and within a few mouths
they were members of his church, on confession
of faith in Christ. He had won the whole family
for his Master by a smile. There *is* power in *love;*
and its sunshine should illumine the world.

I was now satisfied with my acceptance, and believed that my sins were blotted out. The "almost persuaded" was exchanged at last for the
"fully persuaded." I *knew* that I had passed from
death unto life, and that I was a child of God.
Blessed assurance, the value of which to me could
not be expressed by mountains of silver and hills
of gold. I had what the world had not, and what
the world could not bestow. The sweet hope of
childhood had been long deferred; but it was realized at last in early manhood. Why I had not before fully surrendered was, and must continue to
be, the great mystery of my life. But I could now
sing, "Saved at last;" and my soul rejoiced greatly
and gratefully in the song.

For several days I remained at Mr. Vandersloot's, attending the meetings of Mr. Welch at night, and greatly enjoying them. Finally, Mr. Welch proposed that I should unite with his church. I said, "I can not, as in all things I do not indorse your belief as a people." "That shall be no bar to our fellowship," said he. "Accept a home with us for your safety and help, and when hereafter you find a home more suited to your convictions and feelings we will give you both a letter and our blessing." From such professed fellowship I could not withhold my hand, and I gratefully accepted a home in St. Pauls Methodist Episcopal Church, of Philadelphia.

Connected with this church was a body of some thirty young men, called "St. Paul's Band," into which I also entered as a member. They held a social meeting on Sunday evening before the sermon, and then again on Monday and Saturday evenings. On Monday evening they planned and divided up their work for the week, which was reported to the band on Saturday evening. They had various small committees, to visit the sick, the poor, the slums of vice for young men, to hold cottage prayer-meetings with the aged, etc. This Christian band saved many a young man, and did a vast deal of good, more than either tongue could tell or heart on earth could know. During the week I was engaged in canvassing, returning, however, to the city on Saturday evening. From my condition and occupation I was expected to take little work with the band; but their reports and church-meetings were very enjoyable and refreshing to me.

I had informed my home friends by letter of the change in my life, but did not for many weeks venture to visit them. I very much desired to do this, but felt too weak to face my old companions. I knew how fully I had harmonized with them, and something of the social and moral power they could exert over me. I could easily avoid the old comrades in the city, but those at home I knew I must surrender to or face them boldly for Christ. I finally mustered courage to go home, but timidly took the Saturday evening train, that I might meet none of my old associates before the Sabbath. My father, as I feared would be the case, did not feel satisfied with my having joined the Methodist Church, and felt much grieved that I had not cast in my name and lot with the old family church. From him, therefore, I did not receive the warm encouragement that I needed and had expected. The church is too often first and foremost with man; and our devotion to that of our particular choice often blunts the point of our spiritual power over men.

My mother was of a warmer nature. She expressed great satisfaction at my course, and gave me
warm words of encouragement.

Nearest my father's home was the Methodist
Episcopal church. I knew that before the morning sermon they held their class-meeting, and in
this I determined to begin the work of the day.
It was only for members, as I knew; and when I
entered the room there was an expression of great
surprise. They had heard nothing of my change,
and little dreamed of my relationship with them.
They knew, too, of my former wild life, and wondered why I should come among them at that
hour. As I felt and knew, every eye was upon me. The meeting was wholly of a voluntary
order; and its spirit, compared with that of the
Philadelphia meeting, was one of coldness. Near
the close of the meeting, to the surprise of all, I
arose and briefly related my late experience, and
solicited an interest in their prayers. Many fervent responses encouraged me in my remarks, and
after the meeting many kind and cordial words
were spoken by the various members.

From the class-room I entered the auditorium
for the sermon, taking my seat well in front. After the service I went directly home, without meeting any of my old mates. The reader certainly
will not suppose that I did not feel kindly toward

them, or that my heart lacked love for them. I would have done anything on earth to have led them to my dear and blessed Master. I desired first to be more fully committed to the cause before them, and by public religious devotion. Then I felt that they would accept me as a Christian, rather than as merely one of their old, jovial mates. I determined during my stay to approach them, and if possible win them to the side of Jesus and his truth. Many of my mates were at the morning meeting; but the action in the class having been whispered around, they were a little shy of me, as indeed I was of them, so that we did not meet at church; nor did they call during the afternoon. Few, very few indeed, of the young people of Doylestown, at that time, were identified practically with the work of Jesus and his church.

In the evening I was early at church, and, as before, took an extreme front seat. By the altar and among God's own people I felt most safe. And, indeed, the altar is the place for God's people in the sanctuary. When the heart is warm, as with the young convert or devoted veteran, they *crowd* the altar with their presence. They would get as near to God's own throne and presence as possible. Like true soldiers, they would be at the front. If the church be cold, even professed Christians will linger by the door as though they dreaded the holy, cleansing fire of the altar. There is nothing more encouraging to the minister than to see his own flock gathering about him and around him as he ascends the holy place, and nothing really more discouraging than to see them only at a distance from the center of service. Reader, if you would hold up the hands of your minister go to the front. There the active work is done; there the sinner is born again; there the presence of the Spirit is most manifest.

The minister came in a little late. After opening the meeting, and while the last hymn was being sung, he advanced to me and said, "Brother Smith, I am sick, and really unable to preach. You must come forward and talk to the people. The story of your experience will be edifying to all, and through it you may reach the hearts of the young people." I was amazed at the thought of speaking to an audience that almost literally crowded the house. I had little experience in speaking, and positively declined to accede to his proposition. However, he insisted, and finally, with great reluctance, I consented. After a moment's hesitation, I spoke some half hour to the people with special freedom. A few brief remarks from the minister, and the meeting was closed. I returned home with a refreshed spirit, and felt to thank God that I had so good an opportunity

to commend the name and cause of Jesus to my
dear old comrades. Although wholly unsought,
and as completely unexpected, yet I had the opportunity that I most needed. I had now fully
committed myself to the cause in the most public
manner. My young mates knew from my own
lips what was to be the manner of my future earthly life; and I had invited them and pleaded with
them to come with me to the banqueting-house of
the dear Redeemer.

For a few days my gay companions of other
days rather avoided me than otherwise. When
passing on the street I heard a few purposely loud
remarks regarding my case, and a few that were
specially chilling to my feelings. At the end of
the week several of my old mates approached me
and proposed a glass of lager, and then, on declin-
ing this, a stew of oysters. This also declined,
they insisted on my bringing out my violin as of
other days. However, I felt that to these appeals
I was wholly immovable. If they would approach
me only with such temptations, I was at least safe.
There were those in town whom I dreaded to
meet, from knowing their intense opposition to
religious people, if not to religion itself. Among
those was a German mechanic, whose scathing
talk against so-called religious people I had often
heard. Meeting him in a store one day, the mer-

chant mentioned to him the late change in my
habits of life. "Yes," the German said, "I had
heard of it;" and then, to my surprise, he said,
"Mr. Smith, it is the best thing you ever did; and
the hearty advice of my heart is, 'Stick to your
profession; do not give it up." I was grateful to
the man, and thanked him from a warm heart.
The rough world has greatly more respect for religion than we are wont to imagine. They know
something and much of its worth; and there are
times when they are ready to express their appreciation of it. That the sinner is so ready to condemn the unreasonable life of the professed Christian is no less proof of the worth of religion than
his praise, uniformly, of the consistent life, and of
religion itself. The lukewarm and inconsistent
church-member brings many a wound upon the
cause, and keeps many a poor sinner back from
Jesus Christ.

A few days after I was in a barber-shop, where
I met several old associates. As I entered the
conversation was instantly suppressed, and immediately a young fellow began to preach a take-
off sermon in German. I understood well his talk,
and at first felt very indignant. I thought that at
least I would reprove him for his insult, but then
concluded that as a matter of personal, moral
safety I had better bear all in silence. These in-

sulting taunts and temptations endured but a few days, when they ceased entirely. Satan is not disposed to surrender his servants without a struggle; and he struggled hard, I am sure, to retain me in his service. My companions seeing that my surrender to Christ was both sincere and complete, I was soon safe in that direction. I had fought a severe battle, as I anticipated I must; but by the help of God I had won the day and carried the field. The old idea of preaching, so fresh in the mind of my childhood, now came back to me with great force; at least I would by personal effort seek to bring men to Jesus, and if the way opened for wider work I would be ready to enter it. I made something of an effort among my old mates; but beyond extorting a few good promises I felt that I had accomplished nothing. I now felt that I had fully performed my mission at home. I had confessed Christ at least before my old comrades, and was now ready to return to the city,

On arriving at Philadelphia I opened my heart to Mr. Vandersloot regarding my conviction of duty ministerially. He advised me to continue the business of canvassing for the present, handling the Bible and other good books, and await the openings of Providence. He also at this time gave me much good advice regarding my personal habits, and especially as to the service of prayer. He insisted that I could not be too particular in this direction, and that faithfulness here would assure my success as a Christian. Said he, "Close the day with prayer, and begin the day with prayer. Never seek sleep without therewith seeking God and reposing on him your all. Never leave your room in the morning for the duties of the day without first commending yourself and the directing of your steps to God." More important counsel was never given a young convert than this; and its observance has proved a mine of richest value to me. Too much time can not be given to prayer. Indeed, the Christian is admonished "to watch and pray," to pray always, and in all things to give thanks.

A number of ministers were once discussing different scriptural problems, one of which was, "How can one pray without ceasing?" At length one of the number was appointed to write an essay upon the question, to be read at the next meeting. A lady overheard the proposition, and stepping into the room she said, "What, a whole month's waiting to tell the meaning of that text? It is one of the easiest and best texts in the Bible." Said an old minister, "Sister Mary, tell us what you know about it. Can you pray all the time?" "Oh, yes, sir," she answered. "Tell us how you can," said he. "When I first open my eyes in the

morning," she replied, "I pray the Lord to open
the eyes of my understanding; while I am dress-
ing, I pray that I may be clothed with the robe
of righteousness; when I wash, I ask for the washing of regeneration; as I begin to work, I pray
for strength equal to my day; as I kindle the fire,
I pray the Lord to revive his work in my soul;
when I sweep the house, I pray that my heart may
be swept from all impurities; when I prepare the
breakfast, I pray God to feed my soul with the hid-
den manna." "Enough, enough," cried the old
divine; "go on, Mary, and *continue* to pray without ceasing; and, brethren, let us bless the Lord
for this exposition." The essay was considered
unnecessary.

Why, Pericles, the great Athenian statesman,
heathen though he was, never began to address the
people without first invoking the help of the gods.
The great Roman general, Cornelius Scipio, never
undertook any affair of importance after he became
emperor without having passed some time alone
in the temple of Jupiter Capitolinus. Says Plato,
"The best and noblest action of life is to live in
continuous intercourse with the gods." Even that
distinguished man, John Quincy Adams, never in
his whole life retired to sleep without first repeat-
ing that simple prayer, "Now I lay me down to
sleep," etc. He thought the language eloquent

enough for the world's most eloquent lips. Says Augustine, " When we read God's word, he speaks to us; but when we pray, we speak to God." The conversation should be mutual. If God speaks to us, we should answer him.

CHAPTER XXXVIII.

ON THE ROAD AND IN THE FIELD.

We called on Mr. Welch for counsel, and he advised me to follow the course suggested by Mr. Vandersloot. An advertisement was inserted in the papers for a boy of pious parents to serve as a guide for a blind man. The next morning the very one that I needed came, and I engaged him. He was a good, intelligent lad, and answered every want as far as possible. I stipulated, among other things, that he should read me God's word at least one hour daily. Thus he was to become my teacher, and in no small degree aid me in my preparation for the solemn work of the ministry. From Mr. Welch I also received a letter of commendation, covering my membership with and the fellowship of his church. Taking Mr. Vandersloot's, "Life of Christ," and sample Bibles, I started for the city of Reading, Pennsylvania. On arriving I obtained the names of several ministers, on one of whom I called, that through him I might secure a Christian home. I had hereto-

fore stopped at hotels, but in this habit I was
compelled by my feelings and my personal interest
to make a change. I must have Christian surroundings and retirement, which good private
homes would afford me. My profits were not to
be as large as formerly, but my expenses were to
be less, so that I was to be no real loser in the end.

Mr. C., the minister on whom I called, proved
to be an old friend, and after tea he conducted me .
to a quiet Christian home in the house of a widow
lady. It proved the very home I needed, and for
several months I was happy under its shadow. My
companionship was no longer of a dangerous class,
but one calculated to comfort and strengthen me,
while my sales were of books that I could con-
scientiously commend, and the reading of which
must result in good. Indeed, if I could not yet
preach, I was spreading that word which has
proved the grandest preacher of any age or nation
—the word, the glory of which is as the sun of
day. When an Indian minister presented himself
at the court of Queen Victoria he inquired of her
in the name of his prince, "What is the secret of
England's greatness?" She brought him a beauti-
fully-bound copy of the word of God, and said,
"Present this to your prince, and tell him this Bible is the secret of England's greatness." The
Bible, indeed, is the secret of modern civilization;

and it is the grand basis of the happiness and hope of man.

When my daily Bible-readings began I was astonished to find how little I knew of its sacred lessons. But I was deeply interested now. I had a good reader; and during my three months' stay in the city of Reading I made rapid progress as a Bible student. I was deeply moved, and with each reading greatly comforted. I attended Mr. C.'s meetings, and also class, at his church for some two weeks; but these seemed as coldness in the worship compared with those in Philadelphia, and I hardly felt at home.

One day I met a gentleman who invited me to attend his church and class, which, under his escort, I did that very evening. The minister was a young man but little older than myself, and his people seemed humble and spiritual. A series of revival-meetings were in progress, and these I attended nightly for many weeks. I took a free, active part in exhortation, counsel, and prayer, all of which I greatly enjoyed.

Up to this time I had a clear evidence of my acceptance; and yet I longed and prayed for a clearer light, and, if possible, a higher life. I wanted a higher measure of joy and a deeper measurement of feeling. Others seemed to possess these, and I determined that I would also, if

such possession were possible. One night, about
two o'clock, I awoke from a deep sleep, possessing
such a flood of peace and such a weight of joy as
I had never before experienced. I could not lie in
bed, and felt that I must awaken the family. I
was now possessed of all I longed for. I had
reached perfect trust, and was filled, as I believed,
with all the fullness of God. I felt that I was en-
dued with power from on high, and that God had
now given me a special qualification for work.

The field of moral work, too, was opening and
enlarging on every hand and in a great variety of
ways. The gentleman of the house, a brother of
my hostess, was an active member of the Young
Men's Christian Association; and one Sabbath
morning he invited me to accompany him and several others to the alms-house, a few miles distant.
Here, by request, I addressed the unfortunate inmates, who seemed to accept my words with interest and emotion. I was much blessed by the
meeting. At the close of the service a gentleman
requested me to go into his neighborhood in the
afternoon and address his Sunday-school, promising to come to the city for me if I would do so.
I promised, and in the afternoon accompanied him;
and in my Master's name I addressed the Sabbath-
school with great personal enjoyment and profit.
I also visited the prison with the Young Men's

Christian Association workers, and addressed the prisoners with great liberty, and I trust with some profit to them.

The opportunities for work now daily multiplied on my hands, and came without seeking. But I had thoroughly canvassed Reading, and business required that I leave the city. I canvassed from town to town until I finally reached Williamsport, where I was to remain for a time. I had almost perfect peace since the evening above referred to, while the old feeling of fear which had troubled me so much, especially in traveling, was entirely gone. I felt as safe on the train as within my home or my bed. I was God's child, and lived, I felt sure, under his watchful eye, and in his very arms. Why should I fear while God was with me? He would stand by me, even in the presence of death. Everywhere, too, friends received me cordially, and a thousand courtesies were extended to me. Verily, I shared in every good thing, and lacked for nothing.

On alighting from the cars at Williamsport, I met a gentleman on the sidewalk and asked him to direct me to a Christian home. Said he, "I can take you right to the place you wish." He was a physician; and his carriage being by him I was soon seated within it, on my way to the asylum I had wished—a good Christian home. Our first application was, perhaps fortunately, unsuccessful; but he knew where to make another. We soon reached the pleasant and prettily-located home of Mrs. Harriet Homet, where accommodations were accorded me. I was welcomed by one of Christ's most devoted servants, and one of the most ardent workers of his church. I had truly a delightful home, in an exceedingly pleasant family. I had met, too, that woman who in the providence of God was to teach me the way of God more perfectly—in what manner, and to what extent, will soon appear. As Apollos had reason in after life for thanking God that he had met Aquila and Priscilla, so I have had reason to thank God that I met this "Priscilla" of God's household. The church has many of them, but it has none to spare.

In this Mrs. Homet I felt at once that I could place perfect confidence. Approach to her was with the utmost freedom. Indeed, I had never met one, I thought, whom I could approach so freely. In some ways even my own mother seemed to stand a greater distance from me than she. She was one of those congenial or affinity spirits one will meet a few times in life. Between such spirits there is no barrier. Name, complexion, features, age, or station, neither one nor all, enter into the field of consideration when spirits find their congenial mates. I have no doubt but this

21

feeling of affinity will largely determine our relationships and associations in the other life. That
it does here, we know. But our soul-attractions
and congenial companionships in this life are not
determined by the goodness of those who are
members of our church circle, or indeed of our
family circle, and who are thus bound to us by spiritual or even consanguineous ties. We may sometimes take to the most cordial sympathy and fellowship of our hearts persons heretofore unknown,
and separated from us by the semi-circumference
of the globe. As in this life, so doubtless in the
other. We shall meet angels whose companionship would afford no special attractions or satisfaction to us, while for such a one other angel hearts
might beat in most perfect harmony. It is doubtless well that these division-lines are drawn, and
that these distinct social demarkations are so completely interwoven with the texture of our beings.

Mrs. Homet was a devoted member of the Baptist Church, and had been for very many years,
while her husband was a deacon of the same body.
Although the children were grown and settled in
life, yet the home was by no means lonely; for a
goodly company of boarders were gathered about
the table and the good man's family altar.

Among these boarders were several young men
of Christian sympathies and habits, in whose com-

panionship I took great delight, and in whose moral work I had a liberal share. The *young men* of this age are figuring with wonderful conspicuousness in the grand drama of moral life and work. The nineteenth century seems to be their special age, while the organization known as the " Young Men's Christian Association" is their grand and blessed rallying-center. This organization must be the cavalry corps of the army of our Lord; for, as Thane Miller says, "it is the church on horseback." It is, indeed, wonderfully and unaccountably strange that these mighty moral agencies have been so generally deferred in their birth until this momentous century. It can hardly be that other generations offered no inducements for moral work like our own, for there is scarcely one vice that is peculiar to our own times. Temptations have ever abounded, and moral degradation and ruin have ever been the experiences of the world. Yet to this age belong nearly all the great reformative and philanthropic agencies, without which the moral hands would seemingly be almost idle. To us belong the Sabbath-school, the Young Men's Christian Association, the Bible Society, the Tract Society, the more than eighty distinct missionary societies, the Peace Convention, the temperance organizations, the Prison Congress, and even the World's Evangelical Alliance. No one of these agencies could we spare. What did the fathers do without them? and why were they not born before? What theaters of wonderful usefulness do these organizations, or the most of them, open to the young men of our age!

The young men of Mrs. Homet's home all regarded her with affection, for indeed she was the light of the household to each. Her heart was ever open to him who wished counsel or comfort; and she had a most happy faculty of lifting the clouds and letting in the sunshine. The world can not get too much social and moral sunshine; and when we meet those hearts which serve as reflectors or concentrators of this sunshine, we have met the world's real benefactors. The idea of waiting for sunlight until we reach the other world is wholly preposterous. If a man does not need light in a darkened and strange way, when does he need it? If the soul in sin and sorrow does not need it, what soul does? Too many are contented to wait until the gates of heaven open upon them. But even now the Sun of Righteousness has arisen with healing in his wings; and walking in the *light* we need to have no darkness at all. We are come to Mount Zion, from the brow of which the world witnessed the resurrection and ascension of our Lord, as well as his crucifixion and burial. Life has succeeded death. The thunder-ings of Sinai belong not to the promised land, in which even now we stand; but ours is the glory of a continued transfiguration. If in our pilgrimage we have sorrow, yet Christ is with us as the Light of life, even though we know it not. No Christian should blind his eyes by putting his head into a cloud, while his feet are seeking the proper steps of his pilgrimage. To go blindly in the Christian life is neither good sense nor duty, in this day of blazing moral light. We may hope that the Christian world is getting out of the cloudy valley and upon the clear mountain top of continued triumph

CHAPTER XXXIX.

AMONG THE BAPTISTS.

I had frequent doctrinal talks with Mrs. Homet, and many pleasant Bible-readings. By my request she read to me much bearing on the baptismal question. I had been, as the reader will recall, deeply impressed by the baptismal scenes I had witnessed in my childhood, and especially by those I had witnessed in the Big Neshaminy, at New Brittain. Since my conversion my mind had been much exercised in this direction, and I ardently desired further light. I had talked with several ministers and other friends, but all, thus far, had been pedobaptist; and though they had offered me their aguments, yet I was both unconvinced and without satisfaction. They generally admitted that the original method of baptism as practiced by the primitive church was immersion; but they failed to show me by what valid authority the method had been changed. Interested in baptism as an ordinance of God's house, I could only be satisfied with the correct form of it. I would know how

Jesus was baptized, and be satisfied only with baptism in the same form.

Mrs. Homet did not offer me much argument, but read me the plain word without comment, and directed me to pray over it for further light. She brought me to Jesus and his disciples, and left me in their company for consolation, illumination, and guidance. Up to this time I simply knew that she was an immersionist, and not that she was a member of the Baptist Church. She neither insisted that I should be immersed, nor that I should change my church relationship. Her manner in this regard was not dictatorial, but warm, cordial, and full of love. She would not force me into *her* church, but lead me more fully to Jesus. She was a practical worker, and gave much attention to the Woman's Christian Mission, of which she was an active member. She did not neglect her household duties; but therewith she found much time to wait on Jesus. The first meeting I attended with her was a Methodist social meeting, in which she spoke and showed herself fully alive to the wants of the sinner. I attended with her, also, the meetings of the Young Men's Christian Association, and through her was soon acquainted with the young men of the city, and with their methods of work and the rich blessings flowing therefrom. For some weeks I attended the Methodist meetings only, Mrs. Homet not insisting on my going with her to her church.

One day Mr. Clapp, her minister, called at her home, and I made his acquaintance. Finding him cordial and social, I alluded to my baptismal speculations and misgivings. He said, "I have heard of your trouble." This was not through Mrs. Homet, as I had supposed, but through another inmate of the family. He sought an expression of my own convictions, in which he led me on by a series of questions covering the matter in hand. I told him that to my mind immersion in water was the only Bible mode of baptism, and that as such it was to be accepted as an outward sign of an inward work. He then offered to baptize me if I desired, to which I heartily assented, preferring only that he should not be troubled for me alone. "I would as soon enter the water for one," he said, "as for many; and I am ready to baptize you at any time."

The following Wednesday evening I attended a social meeting at his church, when my application for baptism and membership was presented by Mr. Clapp. By request, I related my Christian experience; and this was followed by a variety of questions propounded by the deacons, covering the general outlines of Bible doctrines and the Baptist faith They took special pains to enlighten me on the duties of a church-member, and as to what they would expect from me as such. And this is a point, by the way, too much overlooked. Membership is too often accepted and tendered as a sort of accommodation to the church, and as merely a place of safety for the converts. That the church is a place for *work*, the brotherhood should emphasize as a special truth. This vineyard one should enter with tools in hands, and with a heart ready for earnest and constant work. The church needs to be regarded more as a field wherein to work, and less as a school wherein to learn. That we *are* disciples, I would have no man forget; but that we are also workers, I would have all Christian men remember. On entering the gate of the vineyard we shall meet a Master who can and will give employment to each. The child, the youth, the man, the aged, the prince, the beggar, the learned, the unlearned, may all work side by side, both as sowers and reapers, and in the end receive the penny. In these times especially both the woman and the child are recognized workers; and herein is a striking peculiarity of the age. Take the women workers from the field, and we should see many idle plows; and take our children from the forefront of battle, and we should lose many a victory.

The following Sabbath evening I went down in-

to the baptismal font, remembering that Jesus had
gone down into the baptismal waters before me.
As I descended the choir was singing,

> "I love to tell the story of unseen things above,
> Of Jesus and his glory, of Jesus and his love."

To my heart the poet sung,

> "Thus far the Lord hath led me on,"

While Peter whispered, "This you do not for 'the
putting away of the filth of the flesh, but the answer of a good conscience toward 'God.'" Once
beneath the water, I was truly buried with Christ
by baptism into his death; and rising therefrom I
felt "that like as Christ was raised up from the
dead, even so [I] also should walk in newness of
life." The sweet voice of the choir saluted me,
also, with,

> "'Twill be my theme in glory,
> To tell the old, old story of Jesus and his love."

These were happy moments with me, as the
reader will readily believe if he has passed through
the same experience. The joy of my heart was
like that I had experienced when the light of life
burst upon me as I was born again. I had answered the conviction of my heart, and was at
peace.

Soon after this scene I was received as a member of the church, having received the hand of
fellowship from the pastor. My church relation-

ship was changed, but my convictions were unaltered. I was then simply what I ever had been in sentiment—a Baptist. No man, probably, had ever been led more exclusively by the Bible than I; and yet this book had led me to where I now was.

For several months I continued to labor with new zeal in Williamsport and other places, as opportunity offered; and many, too, were the open doors for successful work. It seemed to me that the world's one voice was, "Help," and that all my faculties were transformed into "an ear to hear" it. The gate of duty is ever wide open to the worker; and it is unaccountable that so many pass on without seeing it or caring to see it. The world, ay, the church is full of "Levites;" and as ever men are ready to "pass by on the other side." Only here and there the true Samaritan is seen, with ready hand and heart to help with word and sympathy and bread. If Christ could come down from glory heights to the valley shaded with sorrow and covered with clouds, surely you and I, reader, should stop, listen, and help as we pass by the craving, wretched multitude.

I spoke very often publicly; and by the voice of the church I was finally licensed to improve my gift as an evangelist. This was an event in my life, and yet a step wholly in harmony with my convictions of duty. I felt gratified that the church should commission me; and yet I felt positive that God had, before them, commissioned me to the same work. My license greatly enlarged my field of labor. I was really appointed to public work, and the public had more confidence in presenting their claims for my labors. Mr. Clapp, the pastor, received me into very cordial, social relations, and in every way possible encouraged my desire to serve the Master and answer the wants of man. In the direction of dependence I was certainly a Timothy; and in all ways I felt him to be a Paul.

Soon after being licensed I was in Danville, Pennsylvania, and attended worship in the evening at the Methodist church. The pastor was holding a series of meetings, and felt very much worn by his services. During the singing he came to me and said, "Are you not a minister?" I told him I was a licentiate. "Then," said he, "come forward and talk to the people, for I am not able to do so." I consented, and felt much refreshed. At the close he insisted on my preaching in the morning of the next day. I had never gone into the pulpit for a formal sermon; and I felt much reluctance in consenting, but finally did so. The night was one of anxiety and prayer. I dreaded to formally enter upon what I had accepted as a duty and consented to assume as my legitimate life-work. With fear and trembling I went to the house of the Lord the next morning. I had chosen for my text, "I am the door." (John x. 7.) On arriving at the house, I found that two other ministers were present. This but added to my embarrassment. However, I got along as well, or even better than I anticipated, while from the interest of the people I felt that my words had not been wholly without profit. I had now formally preached my first sermon; and thereby began a work which I felt should end only with my life.

This was in the fall of 1871. During the winter I did some canvassing, but my principal work was in the direction of the ministry. Elder Willis, of Philadelphia, accepted a call from the Baptist church of Danville about this time, and immediately began a protracted meeting, in which work I rendered him what assistance I could. This was a very precious meeting, and resulted in some sixty or more accessions to the church.

CHAPTER XLI.

WESTWARD.

Some months before this I had commenced a correspondence with an uncle in the West, whom I had not seen since I was eight years of age. This correspondence resulted in an invitation to visit his home, in Ohio. A visit was promised, but was deferred from time to time. Finally, in the spring of 1873, I made my preparations for a journey and visit to the West. A ride of seven hundred miles brought me, one dark midnight in the month of March, to Bradford Junction, Ohio. In the morning, greatly to my disappointment, I learned that my uncle lived seven miles in the country. The roads were fearfully bad. But I finally obtained a conveyance; and after a really desperate journey of several tedious hours I was at my uncle's door. The home was a plain log-house; and the style of living with the occupants was much after that usual to squatters in the farther West. I was not then expected; nor did they know of my blindness; but with all this my uncle recognized me at once, and the family cordially welcomed me to their home. This uncle was Nathan Martin, the brother of my own mother. They had four children.

When the first day had pleasantly passed, and the time for retirement had come, I wondered if the family were disciples of Christ, or if anything would be said of worship. Like many another professed Christian, I had deferred mention of religious matters until nearly all other questions had been canvassed. I finally said, "Do you profess to be Christians here?" to which my uncle replied, "We were once church-members, but have not been for some years." Too many in going from their eastern to their western home fail to carry with them the tokens of their profession. Thus many are unrecognized as Christians at first, and from timidity and shame continue long years in the darkness of moral death. Only by a public confession of Christ, however, can we share the sweet joys of the Christian life. This is one glory of our religion. It admits of no selfishness. What Byron has happily said of general joy is specially true of the ecstacy of the Christian life.

> " He who true joy would win
> Must share it; happiness is born twin."

A minister was once preaching in an Illinois

school-house, and at the close of the sermon said, "I will not now leave another appointment, but will, perhaps, come again some time." After the benediction a detective, a gentleman of large intelligence, but of careless life, stepped excitedly to the minister and said, "Please, sir, leave another appointment; I see every sign of a revival." The minister was astonished that the strange request should come from so strange a man, and in so strange a manner. He left the appointment, and shortly a great work followed, in which two of the detective's children shared, although *he* remained largely unmoved. In the East he had been a class-leader in the Methodist Episcopal Church. He carried his letter of commendation to the West, but had never used it, nor confessed himself a Christian in profession. Eternity, to such a man, will be full of regrets at such a course, although he may himself be finally saved, "so as by fire."

I finally suggested family prayer, which I conducted, and in which the family heartily joined. This habit I continued while I remained with them; and the old altar thus re-erected has never since been allowed to fall, nor the fire thereon to go out. What a beautiful custom this is, and how evidently is it of divine establishment. To call the family about the altar of prayer for the daily consecration, and there to offer praise and seek counsel before the Lord, is a scene which angels must stop in silence and reverence to admire. If the angels are about us, as I can not but believe,—for, though unseen, they encamped around about Israel,—it seems to me that the chief and most delightsome places of congregating must be by the altar of family devotion. Reader, is it within your province to establish such an altar? Oh, neglect it not; and maintain it while you live. There should be an altar in every home in all the land. But alas! in many a Christian home the voice is not heard at the altar, nor the fires enkindled thereon.

A few days after my arrival we attended a temperance lecture, given by a Quaker speaker, at the school-house near by. A large crowd had gathered; the talk was good, and withal I much enjoyed the meeting. Learning on the way home that there was no church-service in the neighborhood, I proposed to announce one for preaching. This proposition met with great favor from my uncle and his family, and at once the notice was made through the schools. The attendance was large, the attention satisfactory, and another appointment was made. This was followed by others, as often as four or five times a week. These meetings continued for some three months, until June. I now began to feel a longing for home, and I deter-

22   _

mined to go back to my father's house. In due time
I arrived, and found all well and in usual happiness. I spent the summer delightfully among my
friends, and the season was gone long before I desired.

The last of August was arriving; and many letters from the West imploring me to return having
been received, I determined on a second visit to
Ohio. On the way, however, I felt that I must
take in the town of Williamsport, and thus see my
motherly sister Mrs. Homet, my pastor, and other
dear friends. Indeed, I was to meet one on whose
presence I had not counted, and yet the one for
whom I had begun to feel a great and special want.
Some changes had transpired in the home of Mrs.
Homet; but it was yet the dear old home as ever.
During the day of my arrival I became somewhat
acquainted with a Miss M., a lady in whom I afterward became deeply interested. My brief visit
was soon and pleasantly passed; but it was one
not soon to be forgotten. I was being subjected
to impressions which had much to do with my
future. In a word, I was in love. Already the
mystic fires were burning upon the altar of my
heart. Like many another lover, I was going it
blind; and yet I knew that love would not see
even though it had eyes. Why, then, was not I
as well off as the average? However, I supposed

that this flame would soon die out in my heart; and when the hour of parting came I accepted it as really final.

Once more I was *en route* for the West, where on my arrival I found the Sabbath-school I had left still flourishing, and the weekly prayer-meeting, established after my leaving, still maintained with living and growing interest.

A young sister who had experienced hope in our winter's meeting was still rejoicing in her new-found Savior, while everywhere the signs of a coming harvest from the late sowing were apparent. On my return she expressed a desire for "burial with Christ by baptism." Anticipating that such demands would be made, I had presented the matter to the church at Williamsport when I was there. They had authorized me, if circumstances seemed to warrant, to baptize any person giving evidence of Christian acceptance. This request being made by the above sister, Cornelia Elam, on the second Sunday of October, 1874, I buried her in baptism. This was my first baptismal service; and as it was conducted by a blind man, it awakened a great interest and an extended curiosity. For miles around the farmers were coming early to the baptismal waters; and though the crowd was large, yet it was respectful and silent. The place of our baptism was a point on the Stillwater, overlooked by a bold bluff on the west. The situation was delightful, and the view all that could be wished.

Two weeks later we repaired to the same place again, when I baptized my cousin, Miss Anna Martin. Thus I was reaping some of the fruits of the spring-time sowing, realizing that in truth if the bread was cast upon the waters it should be gathered again after many days. This may not always be realized, even as soon as in my case. Many a time the hand that sows is crumbling back to dust before the harvest-hour is reached. Thus sometimes "one soweth, and another reapeth," and even that whereon he had bestowed no labor. But "he that soweth and he that reapeth" are all of one; and it matters little which part each may take. We should not fail to remember that we are all sowers and reapers. As sowers, we should seek the word for our seed and the heart for our field; while as reapers, we should gather into the heavenly garner. Montgomery, with his eye on Ecclesiastes xi. 6, has beautifully sung:

> "Sow in the morn thy seed,
>   At eve hold not thy hand;
>   To doubt and fear give thou no heed,
>   Broadcast it o'er the land.

> 'Beside all waters sow;
>   The highway furrows stock:
>   Drop it where thorns and thistles grow,
>   Drop it upon the rock.

"Then duly shall appear,
    In verdure, beauty, strength,
The tender blade, the stalk, the ear,
    And the full corn at length.

"Thou canst not toil in vain;
    Cold, heat, and moist, and dry,
Shall foster and mature the grain
    For garners in the sky."

In November I began a series of meetings at the old school-house known as the "Buckeye," where I had been continuously preaching, and where our Sabbath-school and prayer-meetings were held. For three weeks they continued without interruption, and then with more or less frequency until midwinter. I then determined to go East again to attend to two important matters of business. Up to this time ten or twelve had been forward for prayers, some of whom had been hopefully converted God

CHAPTER XLII.

MARRIAGE, ORDINATION, HOME IN THE WEST.

I proceeded to Philadelphia by way of Williamsport, where, on January 4th, 1875, I was married to Miss M., as had been before arranged. Following this event we returned to Williamsport, where the church was called together to decide on my application for ordination. After a sermon from the writer, the church, by a unanimous voice, decided to call a council of ordination. The council came promptly on call; and after the statement of the pastor, covering my standing and ability as a workman, I was called on for my experience both as a Christian man and a minister. This was followed by a general examination, covering Bible doctrine and the usual teachings of the Baptist Church. I then retired, and the council decided on my ordination, which transpired the same afternoon. The occasion was one of profound solemnity to me. I felt that I had before been called of God; but now God's called men, as by his appointment and in his established way, were to participate in my further consecration to the holy work of the ministry. I was to be placed more fully upon the altar, with most solemn ceremonies. Though I had consecrated myself to the work, yet now I felt that I was receiving a second consecration. There was a cloud of witnesses, both below and above; and their mutual fellowship and united benedictions were being extended to me. With the rest, there was the new anointing of the Holy Ghost; for God was present with us to receive and bless the offering.

Following my ordination we started at once for our home in Ohio, from which I had been absent but two weeks. I at once resumed my meetings, and soon baptized, at the same old consecrated spot, four candidates, and shortly after three more, one of whom was my own wife.

In July the marriage of my cousin, Miss Anna Martin, to Allen Kephart, transpired. This was my first wedding. On the same day we organized the fruits of our revival into the Pleasant Hill Baptist Church. In the fall of this year the church lost two of its valuable members by death. The first was Mrs. Martha Blake, a lady of rare Christian worth, both to the neighborhood and the church. She, however, was ripe for the heavenly garner, and at death was certainly greeted by the

angels. Miss Cornelia Elam, my first canc
for baptism, was at the above funeral in app
perfect health, but in a few weeks was her
tenant of the grave. She regretted death,
of all because of her invalid sister, for who
her dependence she cared with almost angel
votion. When the summons came, howeve:
was willing to go. Death had no sting for
and she feared not to answer the call. The
less triumph had begun below; and the swee
foldings of her life were a halo of glory t
dying soul. The evening star was to have an
setting, but no cloud was to obscure its final g
The morning star had come up as a harbinge
the sun of a beautiful, blissful existence had
upon her soul.

Thus passed away from earth my first Chr
convert and my first baptismal candidate. If m
has yielded no other fruit than this, yet shall I
feel that I have not labored in vain. To start, or
to help in starting one soul in the pathway of en
life, is a service for which one can afford to pass t
rough way of the mortal life. If I may thus
blessed one, I am glad that I was born, even th
in darkness I must grope my way to the
Hereafter I shall see; and in the firmamei
glory this dear sister shall shine as a star fo
and ever. As the golden sunset reflected its st

of beautiful light upon the earth, that mortals might see the open gates by which it entered the new world beyond, we gave our sister back to the valley out of which, in the physical, she had come. But only in the physical did we inter her there. The spirit had returned to the God who gave it when the death-angel called her name.

We linger a few moments by her grave; and even while the valley clods fall heavily upon the casket hope animates our hearts. Above these sounds we hear the Savior say, "I am the resurrection and the life: he that believeth in me, though he were dead, yet shall he live." And to the church and friends could we say, "Thy sister shall rise again; for the dead, both small and great, shall stand before God." Bonar says:

"Soon shall the trump of God
    Give out the welcome sound
That shakes death's silent chamber-walls,
    And breaks the turf-sealed ground."

Here we end the story of our life; not with hope buried, but with the thought and expectation of the resurrection near.

CHAPTER XLIII.

FAREWELL REFLECTIONS.

Our story has been told in great weakness, and with commingled grief and joy. We have passed through dark valleys; and anon the mountain-tops have been ablaze with brightness before us, and we have placed our feet thereon. The way, even to me, has been one more of light and triumph than of shadows and defeats. I would not wish to walk the way again, nor to descend into the dark, deep caverns of the route; and yet if I should, it would be with a livelier hope of gaining the hill-top beyond. The valley clouds have never wholly covered me; nor have I ever given over my soul entirely to despair. The light has ever shone, though dim and distant; and the far-off goal has always been reached in good time. Even when sight was gone, welcome hands were found to guide my feet and hearts of sympathy to soothe my sorrow. I could hardly afford to part with any page of my strange experience; for from all I have gathered fruit that has been both refreshing to the soul and grateful to the taste.

This world is one of native darkness. Not one ray of light belongs inherently to it. It is one deep, fathomless sea of gloom. Light comes, but it is from other worlds. The sun illuminates our path by day; the moon and stars by night. Thus, though we are born from darkness into darkness, yet the light has preceded us, and, like a lantern, is continually illuminating the way a few steps before us as we move onward and forward. There are moral lights no less than physical, and together they come from the without, the beyond, the unseen, and the blissful above. Not the light of day nor that of night, not the physical nor the spiritual illumination could we spare. But as the world's natural gloom is illuminated by a foreign and celestial light, so too is the soul's deep moral gloom as evidently thus illuminated. The night of darkness is deep and impenetrable with both. As well blot out the sun and all the stars, and depend ever and only on the flickering candle, as in the mere light of human intelligence. "It is not in man that walketh to direct his steps;" "but there is a spirit in man: and the inspiration of the Almighty giv eth them understanding." In the spiritual world, we who are in the mortal form have ten thousand aids. Some are as brilliant suns, and some appear as but feeble, flickering stars; but with none can we dispense. Every ray of light that falls athwart our way is a needed ray, and will make brighter and more lovely our path. He that said, "Let there be light," will not leave us in the darkness; and in the apparent gloom the Master himself will be very near.

Before closing this book there are a few things in my life which I would gladly emphasize. This done, and I shall take my leave of the reader.

The *wandering spirit*, or the *desire for adventure*, was the ruling and ruining element of my early life. It led me as a child to the battle-field, and as a youth away from home and out upon the water-wave of the sea. It brought me much sorrow and immeasurable suffering, and tipped to my lips at last the bitter dregs of the blackness of darkness in life-long blindness. Did joy come, it was only resurrection-joy, for I was often deeply buried by cruel hands and untoward circumstances. But what infused into my heart this spirit so fruitful of sorrow and affliction? It was the poison of light literature, after which my soul went out as the bee for its honey-bower. Will my younger readers be warned in time, and give not the life to romance and fiction? Even the Sabbath-school is not entirely guiltless in this direction, but is doing a fearful share in poisoning the soul of society. Some of its own literature is actually pernicious, in that it is creating cravings that will be satisfied only by the cup of moral death. Books of a poisonous spirit are bought by the bushel, and are greedily devoured by the armfuls. It is questionable if some and many of our Sabbath-schools would not be even better off if their library keys were lost. That some good lessons are inculcated in the more acceptable forms of literature, we make no question; but it is much as the sugar that serves as a coating for the bitter, nauseating pill. A censor for the press we would not have, for older heads may ˙judge and wisely choose; but for the Sabbath-school literature of the day we would have a college of the most thoroughly competent censors for the sake of our endangered youth.

The reader will also have discovered that my early nature revealed a largely religious tendency. In childhood I longed to be a Christian; and had I been surrounded by fervent, religious teachings and teachers, I should have been early in the fold of the Shepherd. There I would have been safe from many of those influences which led off and down my too trusting soul. Even the man of strength and experience needs the watch-care and protection of the church. Does the child need less than the man? The Sabbath-school, and even the home-circle will not alone answer the full want of the child. As soon as he can be awakened to a sense of his moral obligation he should be infolded in the bosom of the church.

A superintendent in Michigan was telling the children that they should go to Jesus, and rest in the arms of his love, when a little child went forth from her seat, and taking his hand, said, "Please, sir, lead me to Jesus." This is what our children want. Nor should we feel safe regarding them until we answer this want of their hearts.

Spurgeon remarks that during his London ministry of the more than 2,700 members he had received, several hundred were children, and no one that he has been obliged to expel from fellowship was received in childhood.

At a recent New York Methodist Episcopal conference, of 250 ministers, the youngest conversion among them was at the age of seven years, and the oldest at twenty years, while the average was fifteen years. Not only is it possible for our children to be converted young; but it is very necessary, both for their comfort and safety.

A prince, as a child, was manifesting very much concern for his soul, and his attendants tried to comfort him by saying, "You need not yet give attention to these things. Wait until you are older." "Oh," said he, "I have been to the burying-ground, and have measured some of the graves; and I find them even shorter than I am."

A Chicago mother took her two little girls, seven and nine years of age, to Mr. Moody's meeting, and led them into the inquiry-room, where they soon found peace in believing. A year after the mother, with these children, sailed for France; but when within mid-ocean the Liverpool, her vessel, went down. She was saved, but her two children perished; yet they went down trusting sweetly in Jesus. "It seemed to me," said the mother, "when finally saved myself, that God had permitted me to take my children to the gates of heaven and leave them there." Truly, we can not too soon welcome the children to the fold.

As a final thought, I feel safe in insisting that my life has been singularly filled with gracious providences. "Who among men," I am led to exclaim, "has been more highly favored than I." How strangely was I favored upon the battle-field by Lieutenant McCoy! Then, as soon as I was on the boat bound for Philadelphia, what a friend did I find in Dr. Hartshorn! How was I cared for in the hospital, by the nurses, physicians, and even the good friends of the city of Philadelphia! When on board the Vincie, bound for Rio Janeiro, could I have found a truer, dearer friend than Mr. Watson, the New York merchant? See how his goodness, or rather the goodness of the Lord through him, followed me all the way from the day of my landing in Rio Janeiro. Did he not find me a strong friend in the American consul?

Could I recall his name, I would like to print it
in letters of gold. Could a child of sorrow have
found a more blessed home than that offered by
the sisters in the hospital?   In sailing home, finally,
could I have had a better, truer friend than Captain
Thomson, of Baltimore? And was it not strange
that from Mr. Watson's generosity I should at
that moment of separation at Baltimore have
counted a hundred dollars into my own hand?
Welcomed back to the Episcopal Hospital in Philadelphia, how friends gathered about me, and what
sweet words of cheer greeted my ear.   Then, why
should I have interested strange physicians in my
case, and thus have gained admittance to the Institution for the Instruction of the Blind before
my proper time? How wonderful, too, was the
friendship of Mr. Vandersloot, and what a blessing he proved to me in his kindness and Christian
love!   Truly I must say, "God hath led me all the
way."   I see clearly the foul blotches on the tablet
of human character; yet I see great good in the
human heart; and with pride I confess I have great
faith in humanity.   I wonder not that angels hover
over man with interest, nor that Jesus came down
to redeem a wicked and wretched world.

M. Angelo stopped by a piece of marble imbed-
ded in the mud and rubbish of an Italian city and
sought to recover it.   In his humble endeavor he

was remonstrated with. His defense was, "I see an angel in the marble, and with my chisel I would let it out." The chisel of God's truth brought to bear on the human heart will transform it into a living angel of endless life. May our hands be ever ready to use the chisel.